D0580084

nw

DATE DUE   FEB 03

9-14			
GAYLORD			PRINTED IN U.S.A.

READER'S DIGEST

HOME

DECORATING

Reader's
Digest

THE READER'S DIGEST ASSOCIATION, INC.

A READER'S DIGEST BOOK

Designed and edited by Eaglemoss Publications Ltd.

Copyright © Eaglemoss Publications Ltd. 1998
Based on *Creative Ideas*

The credits and acknowledgments that appear on page 192 are hereby
made a part of this copyright page

Front cover: (main picture) Worldwide Syndication;
(top left) Elizabeth Whiting and Associates/Michael Nicholson;
(center left) Eaglemoss/Adrian Taylor; (top right) Elizabeth Whiting and Associates/Brian Harrison;
(center right) Marie Claire Maison/Hussenot/Chastres Comte/Roy.
Back cover: (main picture) Eaglemoss/Lizzie Orme; (bottom left) Eaglemoss/Gloria Nicol;
(bottom center) The Stencil Store, PO Box 30, Rickmansworth, Herts WD3 5LG, UK;
(bottom right) Robert Harding Syndication/IPC Magazines/Country Homes & Interiors.
Spine: Marie Claire Idées/Chabaneix.
Front inside flap: Ikea. Back inside flap: Eaglemoss/Graham Rae.

Library of Congress Cataloging in Publication Data

Reader's Digest home decorating.
       p.   cm.
    Includes index.
    ISBN 0-7621-0105-9
    1. Interior decoration.   I. Reader's Digest Association.
  NK2110.R43 1999
  747—dc21   98-34016

Reader's Digest and the Pegasus logo are trademarks of
The Reader's Digest Association, Inc

Printed in Hong Kong

CONTENTS

Introduction **4**

INTRODUCTION

Daydreaming can transform your home, and having the confidence to embark on the project is all you need to turn your decorating dreams into reality. The key to success is a combination of inspiration and practical help. Professional advice enables you to clarify your ideas by giving you style tips and introducing you to different decorating techniques, and that is what you will find in the pages of this book.

To start with, take a fresh look at existing decorations, furniture, and accessories, and consider ways of turning areas that may be dull or ordinary into stylish features and focal points. Options to think about include stenciled borders and motifs on floors and walls; original, hand-painted *trompe-l'oeil* designs to delight the eye with their clever, fantasy effects; and atmospheric, broken-color paint techniques, to be used as alternatives to expensive wall- and floorcoverings.

Found objects, such as seashells, provide their own inspiration and their sculptural forms make beautiful ornaments – wonderful with marine color schemes. Imaginative tiling ideas give splashbacks and surfaces new looks, and decorative wood and plaster moldings can enhance doors, walls, and even accessories such as plant pots.

Inspiring ideas for making impromptu tables and quirky shelves encourage you to make the most of a little and create your own, individual style. Accessories can usually be adapted to suit any room in your home. Wood and wicker, tie-backs and tassels all deserve creative scrutiny. Some ideas presented here call for simple sewing or woodworking skills, while others require no more than a little patience with scissors and glue.

They will all spur you on to create attractive displays with everyday as well as more unusual objects, and to solve troublesome storage problems with minimum effort and expense.

Choosing the right color scheme can seem daunting, especially if you don't have a clear idea of the effect you are aiming for. Pictures of real interiors show how warm and cool colors create quite different atmospheres; how they energize or relax, and make a room seem larger or smaller. Use a favorite color choice, such as yellow, green, or red, a gentle pastel color, cozy terra-cotta, or graphic black and white, as the starting point for an individual scheme. If you're unsure about a particular color, see how small amounts – used as accent colors – can add vitality to a room.

Your color scheme chosen, you need to decide on patterns for fabrics, wallcoverings and accessories. You could try using differently scaled prints together, or think about combining plains with patterns. Particular pattern "families," such as mini-prints, stripes, checks, tartans, and spots, are worthy of special attention; and, used with flair, bold florals and co-ordinates can produce attractive and unusual effects.

Getting down to practical basics, clear and uncomplicated advice on decorating techniques is essential. Take the view that tackling something new is a challenge and you will find all things are achievable. When it comes to decorating your home, whether you are hanging wallpaper, curtains, or pictures, renovating woodwork, fixing tiles, or simply want advice on choosing soft furnishings and accessories, this book will help you to create a comfortable, stylish place that you can truly call home.

~1~

ADDING
CHARACTER

STYLISH STENCILS

Stencils are the home decorating answer for walls, floors, furniture, and soft furnishings that need a little extra something. Choose a motif that's fun, sophisticated, romantic, or elegant and see how it enhances the look and feel of the plainest room.

There is an enormous variety of stencil motifs and a myriad of ways of using them. They're a great, and inexpensive, way to express your own style, add an individual touch to mass-produced furniture, and soften the look of a bare room.

The right stencil motif helps to create the atmosphere you want, whether you like the country farmhouse look or something more formal or contemporary.

If, for example, you like borders, you can create one from a single stencil: you could repeat a simple one-color image, or build up a continuous design painted in several different colors. A delicate floral border painted on a white wall makes a completely different impact from, say, a gilt, heraldic motif repeated on a dark background.

You can enhance a feature in a dull room by stenciling around it – a frame inside an alcove or a border around a fireplace. Strategically placed friezes can be used to alter the look of an ill-proportioned room.

Use your imagination and transform fabrics, furniture, floors, and ceramics with stencils. Look for attractively shaped furniture and decorate it with stencils to match the patterns on your border, curtains, or fireplace.

Repeating patterns like this can link different features and provide a unifying theme. Try a dolphin or seashell motif beside the bath and around the mirror in a blue-green bathroom. In a child's room, motifs of clowns, rocking horses, or teddy bears can decorate a quilt and be repeated on a curtain border and a painted chest of drawers.

Many people enjoy stamping their personality on the kitchen, where they spend a great deal of time. Here, decorative stencils can add brightness, color, and fun. Geraniums, herbs, or other floral motifs stenciled around a window, on a tablecloth, or a painted dresser can instill a feeling of sunshine on a gray day.

◀ *The soft, washed-out colors of this floral motif create a delicate pattern on a white chest of drawers. Flowers and leaves from the main motif on the side of the chest are used to decorate the drawer fronts.*

▼ *The plain boxy look of this room is softened by pretty stenciled borders. The simpler border on the back wall echoes the more elaborate flower frieze in the front, and links the two rooms.*

Precut stencils, which are available from home supply, department, hardware, and art supply stores are great for experimenting with the effects that can be achieved. They are available in a whole range of different designs, from miniature single motifs to more elaborate continuous borders. Or start with a stencil kit that includes brushes and paints as well.

Once you're used to handling stencils, you can design and make your own with color combinations and motifs that you like. Be bold, be adventurous, and have fun experimenting.

▶ This room was transformed into a picture of Early American simplicity with the looped, brightly colored fruit garland on the wall, which is repeated on the curtain, bed linen, and the cupboard doors.

▼ The delicate tracery of this flower and foliage design complements and draws attention to the intricate patterns on the fireplace.

▶ A garland of strongly defined leaf and flower shapes encircles the rim of a round table. Subtle blues, greens, and golds were stenciled together on each motif. The floor was also stenciled in a leaf motif, echoing the design on the table.

▼ *This intricate design, based on the patterns of a real rug, was stenciled directly onto the floorboards to create a deceptively realistic effect.*

▲ *This single fleur-de-lis stencil shows how a simple motif can have decorative impact. It is stenciled in gold on the outside of the cabinet and, for a surprise touch, as a border on the inside. It also forms a border on the white wall.*

◄ *Glass covers protect candles and magnify their light, making them more eye-catching. You can turn them into even more of a feature by stenciling them with a simple design. Use acrylic or spray paint to stencil on glass.*

PAINTED FLOORS

A decoratively painted floor can have twice the style and impact
of wall-to-wall carpeting, at a much lower price. Paint
your floorboards to match the surrounding decor, stain them in
glowing colors, or choose a clever trompe l'oeil effect.

Transform the cold, worn look of bare floorboards with the freedom of the entire color spectrum by painting or staining your floor. You'll be amazed at the different effects you can create – and for a fraction of the price of carpeting.

Hardware, paint, and home supply stores stock a huge range of hardwearing, user-friendly paints, stains, and varnishes, so you'll be sure to find exactly the shades you need; and because paints are relatively inexpensive, you can repaint the floor whenever you want. Before you begin, examine the condition of your boards. Fill any gaps, nail down loose boards, and remove old nails and finishes.

DESIGN OPTIONS

Painting your floor presents a great opportunity to expand your creative talents. You can treat the floor as a vast canvas, making it an eye-catching work of art. Try stenciling an intricate border around the edges of the floor, and even around favorite pieces of furniture, so that they stand out more. Stencil a matching motif centrally or repeat it across the boards, and

▲ These kitchen floorboards have a clever trompe l'oeil design of gray and cream stone flags, with corner inserts of rich terra-cotta. The effect is one of rustic simplicity, which suits the style of a working kitchen perfectly and will camouflage spills and stains.

▼ The bold color scheme of this handsome bedroom is followed through with conviction on the floor – the boards are randomly painted in a series of complementary and contrasting shades from the fiery side of the spectrum.

enhance the overall effect with hand-painted details. Finish with a few coats of varnish to protect your work.

Floorboards, themselves, offer a useful series of straight lines, which you can use as a base for geometric designs, such as stripes and checks. Try painting each board in a different bright shade for a multicolored look – a fun idea for a playroom or child's bedroom; or alternate between two complementary colors found in the curtain or upholstery fabric. For a parquet effect, stain the boards with alternate wood stains, then repeat the stripes at right angles, creating a subtle woodblock design. For geometric designs such as these, measure the room and plan your design to scale on paper first.

TROMPE L'OEIL EFFECTS

Virtually any wall-painting technique can be applied to the floor, so you can try your hand at faking handsome marble or rustic terra-cotta slabs, interspersed with delicate, hand-painted tiles. Add a playful detail with the look of a stenciled rug placed under a coffee table or running down the center of a hallway.

If you're feeling really inspired, play more elaborate trompe l'oeil tricks, such as painting a pair of slippers on the floor by the fire, or a casually strewn bunch of meadow flowers by the garden door.

▲ *Fool your friends by stenciling a mock rug on the floor – at least no one will trip over it! The style and colors of this kilim rug complement the soft tones and decorative finish of the country sideboard.*

▼ *Enhance a stairway with a clever paint effect. Here, attention is drawn to the vertical plane of each tread with a stenciled Chinese ornamental design in a golden stain against rich, dark wood that echoes the wall border.*

◀ *Stencil a simple border onto your floor to define the shape of the room. This pretty, powdery blue border echoes the stenciled oilcloth mat in the adjoining room.*

▼ *In this serene dining room, the splendor of a beautifully laid wooden floor is emphasized with a clever painted design. Concentric square sections of the floor stand out in rich blue paint, contrasting sharply with the pale blond of the wood. The decreasing size of the squares focuses the eye on the central dining table, giving the room a pleasing symmetry.*

HARVEST HOME

Use fruit and vegetable motifs throughout your home to evoke
a fresh and natural mood with a hint of fun. Make use
of harvest-print fabrics and wallpapers, together with chic
accessories, from fruit finials to vegetable-shaped dishes.

◄ *The tiles on this kitchen wall are of different yet complementary designs. In a brighter, modern kitchen, opt for boldly colored fruit tiles, showing rosy red apples or zingy yellow lemons.*

▼ *Use a richly colored fruit-print fabric to make a cheerful lampshade for the living room or bedroom. This fruit shade is paired with a light wood base to emphasize the natural theme. You could create a similar effect by stenciling fruits onto a fabric or paper shade.*

◄ *With their vibrant colors and interesting shapes, fruits and vegetables are popular embroidery motifs. Here, ripe figs were split-stitched onto a simple checked tablecloth.*

ruit and vegetable motifs are an especially appropriate choice for the kitchen. In fact, they are a classic design for all sorts of kitchen decoration. Cover the walls with fruity-themed tiles or a vegetable-print wallpaper. Use a bold harvest-print fabric to make a blind and matching kitchen accessories, such as oven gloves, an apron, and placemats. If you don't want to redecorate completely, simply stencil a fruit and vegetable border onto plain kitchen walls, and repeat the motifs on cabinet doors.

You'll find plenty of crockery with a fruit and vegetable theme; display it on a kitchen hutch or wide plate rail when it's not in use. Look for crockery shaped like fruits and vegetables, as well as for china painted with their images; large salad bowls shaped like half-cabbages are popular, as are tea-pots shaped like apples or oranges, with matching cups and leaf saucers.

THROUGHOUT THE HOME

Fruit and vegetable motifs will also add a whimsical touch to the dining room. For an elegant dining room, choose finely detailed fabrics and wallpapers of fruits and flowers in muted autumnal shades or restful pastels. Pair them with fine porcelain painted with dainty berry motifs and create a table centerpiece with a bowl or platter of realistic ceramic fruits.

In a less formal dining room, use bright, bold fruit and vegetable prints, alongside wooden furniture. Set the table with chunky, painted crockery and add some accessories, such as papier mâché napkin rings shaped and painted like colorful fruits and vegetables. You could also try your hand at stenciling fruit or vegetable designs onto wooden chair backs.

Continue the theme in your bathroom by filling a bowl with scented fruit soaps, or have a basket of fruit-shaped sponges on a shelf. You can buy them from a bed and bath shop.

Hang a set of fruit or vegetable prints on the wall in the living room, and continue the theme with tapestry cushions, like the cauliflower and pea-pod ones shown on the next page.

For a delightful cottage look, full of fresh country charm, use fabrics and wallpapers with dainty prints of fruits and flowers in your bedroom.

▶ *Many fruit-print fabrics and wallpapers are bursting with color, making them an excellent starting point for fresh and lively color schemes. In this airy breakfast room, cheerful red checks on the cushions, mug, and napkins; a multi-colored, striped rug; and a blue-and-white leaf-print cushion all echo the bright colors of the fruit-print drapes, cushions, and tablemat.*

▼ Watch for tapestry kits with a fruit and vegetable theme, like this delightful set of cauliflower and pea-pod cushions. The tapestries are satisfying to work, and they look terrific in the kitchen or living room, as chair seat covers or cushions.

▲ This exquisitely detailed vegetable-motif wallpaper is a good choice for the kitchen. It makes an appropriate background for a shelf of vegetable-print crockery.

▼ Ceramic fruits are great fun to have in the home. The salt and pepper pots fit together to make a whole apple.

PRINT ROOM EFFECTS

Revive an elegant tradition in your own home by decorating
painted walls with copies of early engravings. It's an inexpensive
way to give a period flavor to a room, or to transform a
patch of wall space into a treasure trove of fascinating images.

Covering a wall with prints and engravings pasted straight onto painted plaster became a fashionable decorating trend in Georgian times. Formal, symmetrical arrangements were often surrounded by hand-painted borders or similar embellishments – a graceful arrangement of flowers and leaves, perhaps, or a decorative flourish of ribbon to mimic the elaborate hanging of real pictures.

Using a photocopier, it is easy to reproduce this look at a fraction of the cost of buying genuine prints. You can enlarge a small illustration from an out-of-copyright book to exactly the size you want – or watch for postcards, greeting cards, or wrapping paper that have suitable designs – then add ready-made borders and arrangements to create an elegant frame for the design.

◀ This collection of family photos has been built up into an attractive display, using a clever mix of real and illusory framing.

▲ Pasted-on prints can be just as effective on a screen as on a wall. Here the technique has been brilliantly used to link together a glowing apricot wall and a vibrant red screen. Borders can also be used to make frames for the prints or to define a small area of wall decorated in print room style. For an authentic, sepia look, paint the prints with a wash of cold tea or diluted brown paint.

◀ A stunning arrangement of prints like this can cost next-to-nothing; photocopies will do the trick just as well as valuable early engravings, so search your library for out-of-copyright books containing engravings of classical treasures, perfect line drawings of buildings and monuments, and architectural plans and diagrams. The glossy crimson of this dining room wall creates a rich backdrop for the cool classicism of the print display. The prints are elegantly linked by trompe l'oeil rope-and-tassel picture hangings.

BORDERLINES

Line up new looks for your rooms with clever wallpaper borders.
There are borders for every style, and you can use them
to improve the proportions of a room, link colors and patterns,
and add interest or a touch of whimsy to plain walls.

When it's time to give a room a face-lift, wallpaper borders are the perfect quick solution. You don't even need to redecorate the room; borders can be adhered to any sound surface, provided it isn't heavily textured.

If you are considering a complete room change, then think how a border can make the most of its good points or modify any bad ones.

Borders can emphasize traditional architectural features such as chair rails or coving; in modern homes they can imitate them. Remember that borders used like this can alter a room's scale and proportions: for example, a border at picture rail height helps to make an over-high ceiling look lower.

The most straightforward way to use a border is to place it parallel to the floor or ceiling, but there are lots

▲ *A wallpaper border placed just above a wooden chair rail helps to call attention to the rail and links the color of the paper on the lower part of the wall with the main wallpaper above.*

of other ways of using them. Try outlining a fireplace or door frame, create mock panels on a wall, or use them to highlight angled attic ceilings or unusual window frames.

Borders are available in a huge variety of styles, designs, and color combinations, so they can offer something for every decor. Simple, narrow borders look modern and are particularly successful on a plain painted wall. Try a plaid or a check pattern to give a cheery look to a workaday kitchen. Or use bold picture borders as fun friezes for playrooms or children's bedrooms. If you like the highly decorative Victorian or Edwardian styles, borders are a must. You'll find an enormous range of traditional designs.

Details of how to cut and hang wallpaper borders appear on pages 170–71.

◀ *Use wallpaper borders to link your pictures with the room scheme. Here, a picture frame has been painted in the same soft blue as the chair rail, and then a strip of the wallpaper border has been pasted on top, covering the center of the wooden frame.*

▲ Empty jars can be turned into useful storage containers just by soaking off the old labels and replacing them with stylish wallpaper borders. If the jars have glass stoppers, paint the inside of these with ordinary acrylic paint to match the paper borders or the colors of your kitchen.

▲ Wallpaper borders look great at the top of the wall, where they are a striking alternative to plaster cornicing.

◄ Instead of stopping your wallpaper border at the door, take it up and around the door to create an attractive frame. This border picks up the floral theme of the bedroom beyond.

▼ White, flat-packed hat boxes are inexpensive and provide practical storage. Give them an exclusive look by wrapping them with a wallpaper border. This will also cover any ugly brand labels.

▶ *This pretty pastel border is edged with loops like a fabric ribbon. Its attractive check will blend equally well in a modern or traditional home, and it's subtle enough to be used several times on each wall.*

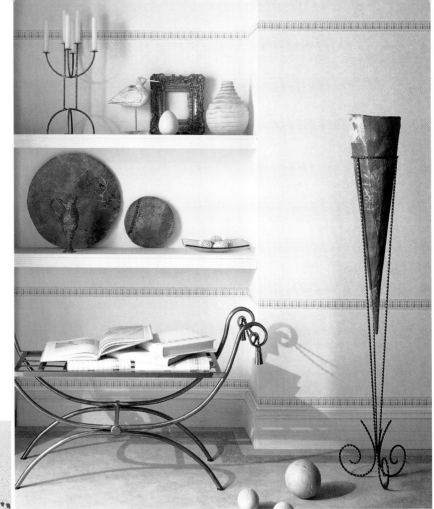

▼ *Children love bright colors and bold prints, so you can really go to town with the wallpaper borders in their rooms. Choose one that features their favorite theme, whether it's animals, trains, cars, or nursery characters. If you're using two different borders, try to coordinate their colors, as shown here.*

▼ *Instead of throwing away all your old tins, jars, or tumblers, you can put them to good use as pencil or kitchen utensil holders. Cover the outside with a wallpaper border, then paint the inside with metal paint for a neat finish.*

BEACHCOMBING

Bring the freshness, tranquility, and tang of the seaside
into your home by decorating it with shells, starfish, and
pieces of driftwood – with their subtle colors and
lovely contours, you can use them anywhere in your home.

Shells always look appropriate in the bathroom, but their neutral, pastel colors and varied shapes and shades can be used anywhere in the home. With their elegant curves, they make lovely ornaments, whether they are gathered together in a jar, clustered in a basket, or placed singly on a shelf.

You don't need exotic shells to make an impact; even mussels and limpets, arranged symmetrically, look attractive on picture or mirror frames. The inside of a mussel shell, for instance, is an iridescent blue, which looks lovely in a

◄ *Cover a wooden box with a variety of shells or simply crown a large crate or trunk with a single fan-shaped shell.*

▼ *Shells are everywhere in this seaside setting. Large shells are combined with tassels on the side of a pot, while smaller ones are used on the lamp base, jug, and basket, and even crammed into glass jars on a high shelf. The smallest shells are glued onto a board and then framed to make attractive and unusual pictures.*

bathroom. So, after serving mussels at a meal, clean all the shells thoroughly and add them to a display. Mother-of-pearl shells have holes down one side and make excellent soap dishes – any water will run out of the shell, instead of gathering in the base.

Seaside towns and beach resorts are the obvious places to look for shells and starfish. When you're on vacation, comb the beaches for shells that have been washed up with the tide; even lots of small shells, displayed together, can look impressive.

Beachcombing is not only fun, but it's kind to the environment; if you gather shells that have been washed up on the shore, you are unlikely to damage the sea life. Many department stores and specialty shops now sell shells as decorative or functional items, but before you buy any, make sure that they have been collected without endangering any sea life.

▶ *Giant nautilus shells make a great start to a collection. Place them singly on shelves for impact. Small shells should be grouped together.*

▼ *Glue a few shells onto the front of a terra-cotta pot for decoration and use it to store a hairbrush, toothpaste, or soap in your bathroom. Continue the theme by stenciling a shell motif onto thick fabric tape and using this to trim your towels.*

▶ *Emphasize your shell theme by using tiles and wallpaper borders with shell motifs.*

CLEANUP

Shells that you collect yourself will need to be cleaned thoroughly. Soak them in a bucket of soapy water – dish-washing liquid is ideal. Scrub them gently with an old toothbrush and a little bleach to get rid of stubborn bits of weed and algae.

▶ *Add a colorful touch to a plain white bathroom by stenciling a shell border above a tiled splashback and along the lower edge of a blind. Two shells on the windowsill and a shell-shaped bar of soap on the basin provide the finishing touches.*

▼ *A wooden fireplace surround, painted in a wonderful rich turquoise, is the perfect setting for a collection of stones, shells, and driftwood.*

▲ *Shells look wonderful set against natural materials like wicker, cane, or bleached wood.*

Paint Magic

Use decorative paint effects to give your walls, furniture, and accessories a stylish and professional finish. Choose broken-color techniques, such as sponging, stippling, or ragging, or try your hand at sophisticated marbling.

Decorative paint effects are an alternative to expensive wall-papers and floor coverings, and will transform plain pieces of furniture. Sponge a dull wall with clouds of color, create eye-catching, textured patterns on worn floorboards with a combing effect, or give an elegant look to an occasional table by marbling it.

You'll find most paint effects surprisingly easy to achieve, using just a few basic materials. They're also easy to adapt, should you decide that you want a darker, lighter, warmer, or cooler effect. For example, you could cool down a sponged yellow and apricot wall by lightly sponging on a pale gray-blue, or you could spice it up with touches of hot terra-cotta.

Decorative paint effects are created by simply applying one or more colors over a base color, so that they form a pattern. In dragging, the finely lined pattern is created by the bristles of a wide brush, while the soft clouds of sponging are formed by a natural sponge. The result is a blend of colors and shades that softens the painted surface and is far easier on the eye than a uniform block of color.

There's a paint effect to suit most tastes and settings. Some of them are very discreet, as in the tiny flecks used in stippling and the watery, dappled finish of color-washing. These are a good choice for bedrooms and for rooms in which you spend a lot of time, such as the living room. Others, such as ragging and combing, have striking patterns that will really make an impact. These are fun, but can be hard to live with, so either use discreet colors or keep them for the lesser-used rooms. Sophisticated paint effects, such as trompe l'oeil marbling and dragging, are an excellent choice for a formal dining room and well worth the extra effort.

▲ The walls of this cheerful dining room have been dragged in medium green over a warm buttermilk base. To create a unified look, the paint colors were chosen to emulate the natural wood tones and forest green of the furniture.

▶ The discreet, mottled effect on this wall has been created by applying a medium yellow glaze over a paler yellow base, then stippling it with a brush to reveal fine flecks of the underlying color. Stippled walls suit any setting and make a flattering, unobtrusive background for most styles of furnishings.

▲ Sponging is one of the quickest and easiest paint effects to master, and you can use it to create different looks, depending on the colors you use. The walls of this airy kitchen have been sponged using two shades of blue for a fresh and restful feel. You could create a similar effect by stippling with a large brush.

▶ Use decorative paint effects to give old pieces of furniture a new lease on life, or to match them to a new color scheme. This grand old wardrobe has been color-rubbed with green over a cream base, softening its lines and giving it a comfortable, informal air that's ideal for the garden room.

▶ A marbled bowl filled with paint-effect eggs makes an eye-catching display. These eggs have been sponged, color-rubbed, or crackle-glazed, and two have been finished with a glossy coat of varnish. Before you begin to paint, pierce a hole in the top and bottom of each eggshell and blow out the yolk. Rinse and wipe dry.

◀ The white walls of this modern study have been spattered with flecks of gray paint, creating a lightly textured background for the sleek furniture and picture frames. The spattering also helps camouflage the radiator.

▼ The walls of this pretty nursery were painted white, then sponged in pink and combed to reveal lines of the white base color. The sponged top color softens the overall effect of the combing to suit the style of the nursery.

ON THE TILES

For a wall and floor covering that's both practical and stylish, you'll find ceramic tiles hard to beat. Use them to create colorful work surfaces and splashbacks in kitchens and bathrooms, and for handsome flooring anywhere.

Ceramic tiles are a practical and attractive covering for walls, floors, and many other areas such as worktops, sink and stove splashbacks, tabletops, windowsills, fireplace surrounds, and hearths. They're hardwearing and resistant to water, steam, heat, and stains, making them the perfect choice for any surface that gets a lot of daily wear and tear,

especially in kitchens and bathrooms, where moisture can make paint flake off and wallpaper peel away.

There's a huge range of ceramic tiles to choose from. You can buy them plain or patterned, glazed or matte, with a smooth or textured surface, or a relief design, and in all sorts of different colors, shapes, and sizes. Many manufacturers sell coordinated ranges

of tiles. You can also buy decorative tiled panels or murals, made up from several printed or hand-painted tiles that you put together to build up a larger picture or design.

You'll find a good selection of tiles in hardware, tile, and home and building supply stores. Make sure your choice of tiles is suitable for the area you are tiling.

It's possible to use ceramic tiles to brighten up the outside as well as the inside of buildings. Use tile adhesive to glue the tiles onto the front of a straight-sided window box, and add a border of white-painted wooden beading for a neat finish. Check that the tiles are fixed on very firmly. If you are going to keep the window box outside year round, use outdoor tiles; otherwise frost may crack them.

Make the most of plain or lightly patterned tiles by laying them at unexpected angles.

If you're going to use terra-cotta tiles on your kitchen floor or worktop, check with the manufacturer to see if you need to seal them to make them nonporous. This helps prevent staining.

▲ Here, a handsome set of Victorian tiles in soft, muted shades has been used to decorate the front of a plain, wooden window box.

◄ In this hallway, speckled, slate gray floor tiles are laid diagonally over the center of the floor, and their layout is emphasized by a border of dusky pink tiles, laid at right angles to the walls. The mottled pattern on the tiles adds texture to the room's simple pink-and-gray color scheme.

► *Crudely painted terra-cotta tiles make a colorful and hard-wearing tabletop surface that's perfect for this country kitchen. Terra-cotta tiles give a warm glow to any room, especially when they're teamed with the honey tones of light wood, as they are here.*

▼ *Two tiled panels with a highly ornate design add a handsome flourish to this white-tiled splashback. Each panel is made up of four tiles that fit together to form the pattern.*

TILES ON A BUDGET

There are all sorts of stylish tiling options even if you've got a tight budget. Try decorating a few inexpensive, plain tiles with stenciled motifs, and use these either as a border or mix them at random with plain tiles. Alternatively, fix plain tiles to the wall with colored grout for a striking grid effect; or arrange the tiles in an interesting way – square tiles can be laid diagonally or stepped like bricks.

Another option is to invest in a few handsome, good-quality tiles and to set these against a plain, tiled background. Watch for exquisite, hand-painted, Victorian-style tiles, which are particularly attractive against a neutral background.

◀ Copies of traditional Victorian tiles have been used to embellish the surround of this reproduction fireplace and to create a handsome hearth in front of it. Tiles are popular for decorating fireplaces because they're heat resistant, hard-wearing, and easy to clean.

▼ The edges of these sink unit tiles were painted in pastel shades before they were fixed in place. It's an easy idea to copy: before you start painting, mask each tile, placing the tape slightly in from each edge and parallel to it, to ensure a straight line. This is a great way to smarten up inexpensive, plain white or cream tiles.

▲ This charming tiled splashback was formed from a hodgepodge of rustic, handcrafted tiles with a cream, blue, and green color theme. If you want to mix together different tiles in this way, make sure they're all the same size and roughly the same thickness.

DECORATIVE MOLDINGS

Use decorative moldings to add character to your home.
You can create elegant paneling on walls, doors, and ceilings;
smarten up rooms with sleek chair and picture rails;
and use small, ornate plaster moldings to embellish furniture.

For centuries decorative moldings have been used to add character, elegance, and decorative flair to interiors of all kinds. In fact they are still a great asset in modern homes, where plain rooms often need a helping hand – just adding a chair rail or a picture rail and some simple coving can make the world of difference to bare walls.

The most popular moldings are cornicing and coving, which give a smart, neat finish where the walls meet the ceiling; baseboards, which do a similar job where the walls meet the floor; chair and picture rails, which break up plain walls into pleasing proportions; door and window surrounds, to highlight and outline these features; and panel moldings and ceiling roses.

You'll find moldings in all sorts of styles, from the highly ornate to the most basic. Decorative moldings are made from wood or plaster, or from a lightweight and less expensive plaster substitute, such as polyurethane or the very economical polystyrene. Lightweight moldings can simply be glued in place, but heavier, plaster ones need to be glued and screwed on.

38

► Before being fixed in place, the moldings on these pale yellow kitchen cabinet doors were painted a bright shade of yellow to make them more of a feature.

◄ These planters have been decorated with wooden moldings and motifs, which were simply glued in place.

►This cast-iron bath has been given a flamboyant finishing touch with an ornate molding glued onto the side. The molding looks like plaster, but it's actually made from a lightweight, plaster-effect material that's much easier to use. The extravagant molding complements the bath's decorative feet, and creates a balanced effect.

Use panel moldings to add smart detailing to plain cupboard, wardrobe, and interior doors. You can buy panel moldings in kits, which are quick and easy to use. Paint moldings a pale shade below a chair rail and a darker shade above it, to provide a subtle contrast with the wall.

A chair rail, splitting the room horizontally as it does, enhances the room's proportions and opens up a whole new range of design possibilities, as you can decorate the areas below and above it in different ways.

▶ *Narrow panel moldings in soft cream add elegance and a touch of grandeur to both the walls and ceiling of this room. For extra definition, the panels are papered with a mottled blue wallpaper in a shade slightly darker than that of the surrounding plain blue walls. Classic cornicing completes the effect; note how the relief design has been highlighted in blue to match the walls.*

▼ *The recessed panels of this sunny yellow sitting room are emphasized by slender strips of panel molding.*

▲Smart panel moldings and a new door surround have turned this plain, flush door into a handsome feature. The moldings are painted in warm yellow so that they stand out, and then, to emphasize the effect, the panels are painted in a lighter shade of yellow.

▶ The chair rail shown here has been painted on to make a trompe l'oeil feature, but it's easier and far quicker to affix lengths of chair rail molding to the wall. This chair rail is enhanced by classical wall-paper borders both above and below it.

FIREPLACE FOCUS

Your fireplace can be a beautiful focal point year round.
When the weather's too warm for a roaring fire, fill the grate
with fresh flowers or a display of dried flowers and leaves, or
cover it with a decorative fire screen or a still-life display.

A fireplace is considered to be a great asset these days because it's easy to make it into a really attractive focal point, even if you hardly ever, or never, light a fire in the grate. So make the most of your fireplace for a year-round feature.

The best decorations fill or cover the empty grate. Make sure they suit the shape, size, and style of the fireplace, and the room it's in. An impressive drawing room fireplace in marble, painted wood, or metal deserves elegant accessories, like a large fan or an exquisite collection of ornaments. If you prefer a cottage look, and your fireplace is made of brick or has a stripped-wood surround, pick up the natural theme with a display of dried flowers or a stack of logs or cones.

FIREPLACE FILLERS

If your fireplace has an attractive surround, or patterned tiles, add a decorative touch that conceals the empty grate without hiding any of the finer points. Arrange plants and flowers in the grate so they spill out of the fireplace without spreading sideways: you can either keep them in vases or pots, or plant them directly into the grate in the same way as a hanging basket, with a tray underneath for drainage. Alternatively, fill the grate with a bundle of twisted twigs, logs, or dried flowers.

A fireplace is also a stylish spot to display a collection of favorite ornaments – china cats and dogs curled up before the fire make a cozy scene. Place the ornaments in front of the grate, or even in it if they fit well, and supplement the arrangement with some fresh green foliage.

If the fireplace is never used and the grate has been removed, you can use it as a storage area. Opposite, an empty sitting-room fireplace has been used to store a wine collection. You could store a basket of towels in a bathroom fireplace, or a collection of cuddly toys or books in a children's bedroom.

▼ *Well-to-do Victorian women used to have fire screens, such as this charming* Little Bo Peep *design, to protect their complexions from the heat of the blaze.*

SCREEN PLAY

If you don't want to clutter up the recess or grate of your fireplace, you can simply cover it with an attractive fire screen, a hanging fabric panel, a painted board, or a large fan or other ornament. If you need to use the fire, you can then just remove the cover and put it to one side. It's a great way to cover up a messy grate that you haven't had time to clean out.

▶ *For a sweet-smelling, economical display, arrange a pile of pine cones in your fireplace. These giant cones have been carefully stacked between the firedogs and a magnificent cast-iron fireback.*

▼ *A defunct fireplace makes a practical storage spot. Here tall potted plants provide a soft frame around the fireplace and partially conceal the wine rack from view.*

▼ *Many Victorian fireplaces have exquisite tiles. If you've got one with tiles too lovely to conceal, you could fill the grate with a few plants when it's out of use. Keep the plants in their pots, so you can simply lift them out when you want to use the fire.*

▲ A fresh arrangement of foliage, Marguerites, and white primulas spills out of the grate of this elegant white fireplace. The grate is planted like a hanging basket, with sphagnum moss, while the mantelpiece is heaped with more plants, draining into a shallow, hidden tray.

▲ The recess of this fireplace is covered with a colorful trompe l'oeil panel depicting a brick recess, filled with an urn, a couple of books, a bowl and other knick-knacks. From a distance the picture looks very realistic.

▶ A cast-iron fireplace makes a magnificent showcase for this collection of exotic ornaments. Here, the fireplace display mirrors the room's black, white, and gold color scheme. Two fragile ostrich eggs lie in the grate, above a sleeping gold cat, while a wooden Dalmatian cutout stands guard to one side. Brass ornaments stand on the ledges above the grate to balance the display and lighten a dark space.

~2~

PRETTY AND
PRACTICAL

COUNTRY KITCHEN ACCESSORIES

Bring country style to your kitchen with a profusion of rustic
accessories. Keep your modern appliances and convenient
layout, but introduce natural warmth with pretty china, flowers,
heaped produce, baskets, and earthenware pots.

When choosing accessories to give your kitchen a country look, think about natural materials. Choose wicker, earthenware, natural woods, or warm terracotta. Traditional metals, like copper, cast iron, and brass are also perfect for the look; so are flowers and jars of homemade produce, and natural fabrics such as pure cotton or linen.

Put fresh and dried produce on display to convey an impression of rural plenty: heap fruit and vegetables in wire or wicker baskets suspended from the ceiling, and hang strings of fresh onions or garlic alongside them.

Display other attractive produce on open shelves, rather than hiding it away in cupboards. For example, fill glass containers with herbs and spices

and arrange them on shelves within easy reach of the stove. Add jars of mouth-watering homemade preserves and earthenware pots of flour, sugar, and biscuits.

Flowers, both fresh and dried, will bring the country into your kitchen. Try hanging a profusion of dried flowers from a traditional clothes rack, and fill china jugs with fresh flowers. In

the summer, add a pot of cheery flowers like geraniums, or choose a fern, which will benefit from all the steam in the kitchen.

Traditionally, china was stored on a kitchen hutch. Hutches can look magnificent and they make it easy to find specific items, but if you haven't got the space for one of these, you could create a similar effect with open shelves. Fix a piece of beading about 2in (5cm) from the back of each shelf, so that you can stand the plates behind it, and screw cup hooks to the underside of the shelves, about ⅝in (1.5cm) from the front edge. A lace or frilled fabric edging, glued or tacked to the front of the shelves, completes the effect.

Bright and cheerful fabrics always look great in a country kitchen, so choose ginghams and checks. For a softer effect, team these with coordinating floral or fruit-print fabrics.

◄ *Display the abundance of your garden produce in a range of country-style containers – sturdy wicker baskets, metal troughs, and whimsical wire baskets.*

◄ *An unusual kitchen accessory with a country motif can form the basis for a collection. A wooden spice rack with a carved-chicken motif was the inspiration for this hen party.*

▼ *A harvest theme print, repeated in the china, table linen, and wallpaper, creates reassuring country warmth.*

If your fabrics have bold country designs, pick up the motifs elsewhere in the room. Stencil them on kitchen units, onto a table, or plain walls, and watch for wall tiles that pick up the same theme.

For the finishing touches, add old-fashioned accessories, like brass scales with weights, and copper or cast-iron pots and pans. Modern reproductions are widely available, but it is possible to find interesting old ones in junk shops and markets.

Collections are always eye-catching, so why not use the kitchen shelves to display a collection of, say, teapots, jugs, or serving dishes. Keep an eye open for pieces with a country feel, perhaps decorated with farmyard animals, fruits, or flowers.

▲ Most kitchen manufacturers include country-style units in their lines, often made in oak or pine. These generally have natural wood finishes, which create the perfect look for a country-style kitchen.

◄ These simple wooden shelves have been given a kitchen-hutch treatment. The pretty "lace" edging is actually a series of matching paper doilies, held in place by the china on the shelves. Instead of using traditional cup hooks to hang the cups, a length of doweling has been inserted through holes in the lower wooden shelf brackets; butchers' hooks are then used to hang the cups by their handles.

▲ *You can do a lot to give your kitchen a country feel by choosing the right tiles. Opt for tiles with country motifs, or in traditional blue and white.*

▶ *Wicker baskets make wonderful storage containers for fruit and vegetables, and can be hung from hooks on the wall or ceiling. Baskets blend beautifully with dried flowers, so hang these nearby, or trim the baskets with a few choice sprigs.*

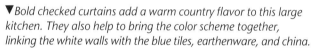

▼ *Bold checked curtains add a warm country flavor to this large kitchen. They also help to bring the color scheme together, linking the white walls with the blue tiles, earthenware, and china.*

TEMPTING TIEBACKS

The simplest curtain treatments are often the most effective, and
nothing could be simpler than pulling your curtains into
shape with tiebacks. They'll give the curtains structure and form
without fussiness, and elegance without excessive formality.

Tiebacks can transform the look of your curtains, sweeping them back into generous folds to frame the window and enhance its proportions. Choose from any number of ready-made tiebacks available in metal, wood, fabric, or cord, or make your own from fabric, strings of beads, or even artificial flowers.

Making your own tiebacks doesn't have to be difficult, although you can go to town with tailored shapes if you wish. A pair of fabric ties, a scarf, or even a necklace can all be used to make quick tiebacks, so even if you're not confident about sewing, you can still create eye-catching effects.

Wood or metal tiebacks. These create a subtle, elegant effect. The metal ones look great used in conjunction with a metal curtain pole or chosen to match any other metal in the room. Wooden tiebacks are usually less expensive than the metal ones, and have the advantage that they can be painted to create any effect you wish.

Cord tiebacks. These come in a wide range of colors and are easy to fit. Usually they are looped over a hook on the wall, but, if you prefer, you can attach them to wooden or metal holdbacks.

▲ *These curtains are permanently fixed at the top, so the tiebacks are placed high to let in maximum light. Each tieback is made from two strips of fabric, bound in yellow and gathered to a metal ring at one end, which is looped over a hook on the wall. The strips are loosely knotted around the curtain to hold it in place.*

◄ *Two strips of fabric, bound along the edges, have been gathered up along the center to create this flamboyant tieback.*

Fabric tiebacks. These come in all shapes and sizes. The standard fabric tieback is stiffened and shaped in a curve that is wider at the center than at the side. This can be trimmed with braid, binding, or fabric frills so that it stands out against the curtains. It can be in the same or matching fabric. Tiebacks can also be made by gathering fabric onto elastic, by making flat strips that are tied in a bow, or by padding fabric tubes and then plaiting them together.

You can give ready-made tiebacks a personal touch by adding a few simple decorations. Braids, cords, and ribbons can be hand stitched in place to define the shape of the tieback, or you can pin or glue on fresh or artificial flowers, beads, fake jewels, or even suitable seashells.

◀ Dried flowers make pretty, everlasting decorations for a tieback – just roll up a strip of fabric, tie it into a knot, and then tuck in the flowers. These are artichoke flowers, which complement the vibrant tartan curtain.

▶ Embellish a plain tieback with shells, spray-painted in bright colors, then glued in place.

▲ These sensational roses are easy to make. Fold a strip of velvet in half lengthwise and trim one end into a curve. Zigzag stitch along the ends and long raw edges, then, with the curve at the center, roll the velvet up into a rose, and secure it with a few hand stitches. The leaves are also made from velvet, with machine-stitched veining.

◀ For festive flair, pin flowers and seasonal sprigs of greenery onto your tiebacks.

▲ Cord tiebacks are readily available in better fabric stores and can often be bought as a set with your curtains. Some, like these, come complete with tassels. As the final touch, choose decorative curtain hooks to hang the cords from.

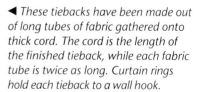

▲ A pair of scarves in complementary colors create an instant tieback. They have a relaxed look, which suits the ethnic feel of the curtain fabric.

◄ These tiebacks have been made out of long tubes of fabric gathered onto thick cord. The cord is the length of the finished tieback, while each fabric tube is twice as long. Curtain rings hold each tieback to a wall hook.

TEMPTING TASSELS

Swinging tassels make charming trims for a whole range
of furnishings. Choose from single tassels in all shapes and
styles to tasseled braids and cords in every color of the
rainbow – they'll add a decorative touch to the plainest item.

Cushions, curtains, and furniture upholstery are the traditional favorites for tassel trims, but you can use them to trim just about anything. Tassels make delightful decorations for solid pieces of furniture and ornaments. You can glue or tack them to the corners of a stool or a chair seat, or drape them around a plain vase. Wherever you choose to apply them, tassels will add visual interest and color.

TASSELS FOR ALL TASTES

Look for tassels in the sewing and notions sections of large stores, in fabric shops, and specialty trimmings outlets. You'll find a huge choice, from dainty or chunky individual tassels in sleek silk or natural cotton, to strings of attractively tasseled braid and clusters of small tassels bunched together.

You'll also see lengths of thick twisted cord finished with chunky, matching tassels – these are designed as curtain tiebacks, but you can use them in lots of creative ways. Silky, tassel-trimmed dressing-gown cords come in many colors and make fabulous tiebacks for fine sheers and for lightweight curtains.

MAKING A CHOICE

When you go shopping for tassels, take a color reference to help you choose, such as a fabric sample. Look for tassels in a complementary shade rather than an exact match; a trim in a different color will look far more interesting, and will introduce a fresh new color into the room.

▼ *Tasseled trimmings give these black-and-white cushions an invitingly soft finish, and enhance the two-tone color theme.*

▼ *You can use tassels as stylish alternatives to plain drawer handles. Simply tie them to the original handles, or remove these and glue the tassels securely in place.*

▼ *Give plain cushions added flair by swirling a tasseled tieback over the front and then slip-stitching it in place.*

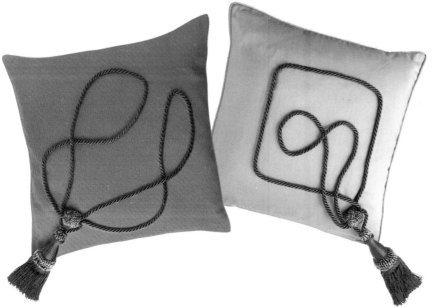

▲ Add decorative flair to a plain vase with a tasseled curtain tieback. Simply slip the cord loops over the vase with the tassel positioned at the front, twist the top loop, and secure it at the back with adhesive tape.

▲ When you look at tassels and braids close up, you can really appreciate their fine detailing. Coordinating braids and tassels are widely available and come in many color combinations.

◄ Gigantic tassels in unbleached natural fibers look spectacular on this outsized damask cushion and make impressive tiebacks for crisp cotton drapes. Combining different textures in this way gives dramatic results, especially if you keep to a simple color scheme.

▼ Tiny keys, such as those used in diaries or jewelry boxes, are easy to misplace, but you won't lose yours if you attach a mini tassel. You can do the same with full-sized keys.

▲ *Give a candle shade the Midas touch by draping a tasseled braid around the top. Make your own tassels by folding equal lengths of wool in half and securing them with tape.*

▲ *A length of tassel-trimmed cord gives a smart finish to this hand-pleated curtain heading. The cord is knotted at intervals across the curtain's width, then looped into a double bow at the center. Matching tasseled tiebacks will complete the stylish effect.*

◄ *A single silky tassel makes an elegant detail on the end of a plump bolster cushion and adds to its luster. A gold tassel has been chosen to highlight the gold stripes in the cushion fabric.*

POLES APART

Whether you're hanging elegant curtains, sweeping sheers, or a decorative panel, the curtain pole is just as important a feature as the fabric. Clever paint effects and finials can transform your window treatment, bringing character and charm to any room.

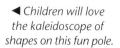

◀ Children will love
the kaleidoscope of
shapes on this fun pole.

Although plain and simple, varnished, wooden curtain poles are very popular, a little imagination can transform them into chic accessories, bringing a touch of style and personality to a room. The quickest method is to echo the curtain fabric on the pole with paint. If you're confident, you can copy the design of the fabric; otherwise, simply paint the curtain rings in the colors of the fabric. For fixed drapes, try wrapping the pole with the curtain fabric for a seamlessly coordinated finish. For lightweight drapes and sheers, experiment with unorthodox rods and poles, such as a length of cane or bamboo.

HAPPY ENDINGS

Finials can be made from large shells, dried flowers, or seed pods for a natural theme, like the plaster starfish shown on the previous page; or use large wooden beads, craft balls, and sawed-off slices of dowel, sanded and painted and strung on coat-hanger wire for an amusing finial to decorate a child's room.

▶ Shelf brackets perform the added
function of holding up a curtain pole in
this clever arrangement.

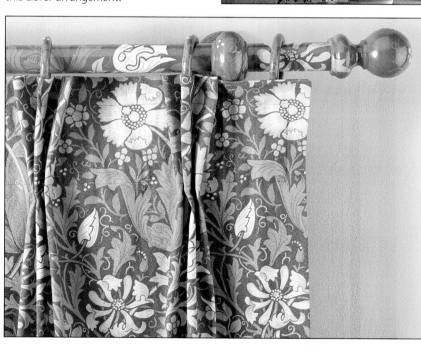

◀ The lightness of simple voile
curtains is perfectly complemented by
a couple of garden canes lashed
together to make this quirky, natural
curtain pole.

▲ This curtain pole has been skillfully
painted to match the flowing design of
the curtain fabric. Alternatively, you
could cut motifs from the fabric and
adhere them to the pole.

PLATES ON SHOW

Most homes have the odd plate that's too lovely or too interesting to throw away. Make a display of your plates by standing them on shelves or hanging them on your walls – they will always be a conversation point.

Every home has a collection of them – odd plates, the orphans of a once-complete dinner service, no longer used but far too nice to throw away. Then there are the pretty hand-painted oddments picked up on impulse at a local school or yard sale, the souvenir of a happy Mediterranean holiday, or that impractical but beauti-ful gift from a friend. Perhaps you have collected plates on a theme for years – floral patterns for the flower lover, pretty salt-glazed stoneware, or ever-popular blue-and-white china.

Here are some of the ways in which you can show your treasures to best advantage. First decide whether you want to hang your plates on a wall or display them on shelves. Plates on shelves are readily accessible, so this is the best method for those that are still in use. Wall fixings, on the other hand, are quite simple to put up, and are easy to change should you want to rearrange the display. Plates displayed on a wall can be enhanced with a decorative bow.

LINKING YOUR DISPLAY

Look for themes to link your collection: it may be color, pattern, or shape. Then consider how the plates relate to their immediate surroundings and what they contribute to the room as a whole. Here you'll find a wide range of possibilities: blue and white china on a fresh yellow wall, a butterfly plate collection framing a mirror, dishes stored on a kitchen hutch ready for use, or simply plates hung to be admired.

FIXING PLATES ON A WALL

There are several ways of hanging plates securely on a wall. The safest fixtures are sprung plate hangers, sold in most hardware stores. Many of the plates shown here are hung in this way. Picture hooks will suffice in most locations, but you may need to use a masonry nail on a particularly tough wall.

Adhesive Velcro tabs are another option, but are best reserved for small plates. The back of the plate must be absolutely flat and, if the wall is papered, you may need to nail the Velcro tab to the wall for safety.

Some souvenir plates are designed specially for hanging – at the back they have a pierced rim through which you can thread picture wire.

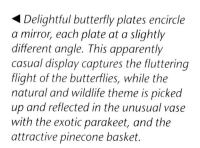

▲ A beautiful old dinner service is displayed on white, uncluttered kitchen shelves. To keep the shelves clear for practical implements, such as pots and pans, the plates are hung rather than propped up on the shelves. The arrangement has been carefully considered: notice the way two dinner plates placed on either side of a smaller plate frame the tureen and emphasize its elegant silhouette.

◄ Delightful butterfly plates encircle a mirror, each plate at a slightly different angle. This apparently casual display captures the fluttering flight of the butterflies, while the natural and wildlife theme is picked up and reflected in the unusual vase with the exotic parakeet, and the attractive pinecone basket.

► *Above the mantelpiece of an elegant fireplace is an ideal place to display your plates. At the center of this display a platter features a subtle relief pattern and an urn of flowers. Around it are six different plates, the blue and white color scheme providing a unifying theme.*

▼ *The addition of a fancy ribbon will turn an ordinary plate into an eye-catching wall piece. This plate is held in place with adhesive discs; the looped bow simply serves as decoration.*

▲ *White walls and curtains can look austere without a dash of color. These plates, reminiscent of ever-popular Delft pottery, provide the delicate and decorative touch that the room needs.*

▲ Neat, pert bows placed above the plate add a jaunty touch to these animal-theme plates.

▲ Here, a splendid collection of dishes, plates, and mugs is shown to advantage against a wall loosely color-washed in bright cobalt blue. The subtle background suits the handmade quality of these beautiful ceramics. The shelving unit, painted a paler, duck-egg blue, provides an effective division between the rows of plates.

PLATES ON A SHELF

Old-style hutches were designed to display plates and had a groove cut into the shelf to stop the plates from sliding forward. If your hutch has no groove, you can create an effective stop by gluing a piece of half or quarter beading about 2in (5cm) from the back of the shelf. If the stop is too near the back of the shelf, the plates will stand too upright and may fall forward if knocked. Also, remember that some plates are bowl-shaped or have a substantial base that makes them quite deep; make sure that you allow for this extra depth.

▶ This set of plates was designed as a wall decoration, since no supports are visible. They fill the space neatly and can be seen as a single decorative element. The fruit theme works well with the floral patterns on the cushions. If your plate collection is to fit comfortably into a decorating theme, you must think of the way it relates to the surroundings and try to find complementary shapes, colors, and patterns.

CLEVER COFFEE TABLES

Instead of installing a standard coffee table, try an original
and creative alternative. You could use a large wicker
hamper, a flat-topped chest or trunk, a well-padded footstool,
or a low piece of furniture, such as a bench.

A coffee table is a real bonus in a living room: you can stack magazines and newspapers on it, serve drinks, or display a favorite potted plant. Good coffee tables can be pricey, but that doesn't mean going without. Try improvising with one of the creative alternatives shown here.

A sturdy wicker hamper or a flat-topped trunk can double as a coffee table and will provide extra storage space for old magazines, books, and toys. You can give makeshift coffee tables like these an attractive finish by covering with a tablecloth.

In a smart, traditional living room, you could opt for a large footstool, upholstered in a stylish fabric. Footstools usually have a firm, flat surface but with soft, rounded contours, so you can put your feet up on them or use them as an extra seat when necessary.

In fact many low pieces of furniture can be used and you can turn the most unlikely pieces into handsome and original coffee tables. If you're short of space, a narrow wooden bench is ideal; or you could use the drawer section from a two-part wardrobe, as shown below.

▲ *A large, well-padded footstool doubles as a useful coffee table in this smart sitting room.*

▼ *The bottom section from an old wardrobe is just the right height, and the roomy drawers provide plenty of easy-access storage.*

▼ *This sturdy wicker hamper serves as a useful second coffee table when the small, round table gets overcrowded. Wicker hampers are inexpensive, and you can spray-paint them to match your other furniture. They're also great for storing table linen.*

STYLISH STORAGE

Well-planned and attractive storage makes a huge difference to any room. Bare surfaces and the absence of clutter create a feeling of relaxation and a comfortable sense of space. Use color, style, and imagination to rethink your storage ideas.

▶ *Solve your storage dilemmas with ingenuity. Here, cubbyholes have been built under the stairs. They're just right for bottles of wine and other small items that can be stowed away.*

▼ *Hats are usually decorative, so why hide them away in a cupboard? Here they're stored on top of the umbrellas and walking sticks in a handsome cane umbrella stand.*

▼ *A stack of huge cardboard tubes makes a shoe rack with a difference. If you can't obtain large cardboard tubes, you could use plastic piping.*

Design is just as important to the look of your home as furniture, color schemes, and lighting. Well-organized storage can transform untidy rooms into comfortable living spaces and turn inconvenient, wasted areas into stylish features.

Look for storage ideas that are both functional and good-looking. They don't have to be expensive – a set of wicker baskets or some painted orange boxes can look just as good as expensive furniture.

USING FURNITURE

If you're short of space, it's always a good idea to choose furniture that includes storage capacity. Beds with

sliding drawers underneath, window seats with storage bases, and chests that form coffee tables can all contribute to an ordered room rather than one with piles of scattered belongings. Chests and blanket boxes can be delightful pieces of furniture in their own right, and you can adapt them to suit all types of room setting. Stenciled designs, or painted or wood-stain finishes can be used to add your own individual style.

SHELVES

From bookcases to kitchen hutches and bathroom cabinets, shelves are a typical way of creating storage space without using up too much precious

▶ Hat boxes always look elegant, and they're deep enough to provide useful storage space for all sorts of things – sewing equipment, trimmings, gloves, or even shoe polish and brushes. Paint the hat boxes in bright colors and trim them with ribbon or cover them in a fabric that will match your room.

▼ This natural wicker basket makes an unusual and attractive container for bottles. To keep your bottles cool, put them in an ice bucket inside the wicker basket.

floor space. The type of shelving unit you choose will depend on your decor, and whether you want the shelving to be permanent or mobile.

Free-standing structures, such as display cabinets and corner units, are adaptable and flexible, and modular units have the advantage of allowing you to expand the space available as your requirements grow.

Built-in shelves are permanent, but a system with adjustable shelves will give some versatility. Alcoves form a natural niche for shelves, or you could put up a few in a corner, which always look attractive. Plate rails, which run around the room at chair rail height, also provide useful storage.

Shelves can look untidy and unattractive if you pile heaps of clutter on them. It's a good idea to store items in boxes or jars and then arrange these on the shelves. Choose coordinated containers.

BASKETS AND BOXES

Baskets and boxes can provide a practical and decorative means of storage. They come in a huge range of shapes, sizes, colors, and textures and make wonderful containers for many things from shoes to toiletries. Try painting them or dyeing them to fit in with your preferred color scheme, and then stack them on top of each other for a neat, well-ordered look.

▶ *For a tidier alternative to the free-standing vegetable rack, fix rectangular baskets onto drawer runners. You can then slide your vegetables out of sight in a kitchen cupboard or pantry.*

◀ *With a system of glass storage jars, you'll never have to rummage through your sewing box for a zipper, replacement button, or length of ribbon again. You'll be able to see exactly what you've got at a glance.*

▶ *Fixing one or two wicker baskets to the inside of your cupboard doors provides extra storage space. Try this idea in hall cupboards for hats, gloves, and scarves; or use it in children's rooms to clear up toys; or in the linen closet, as here. Just fit a metal hook to the door and hang the basket from it.*

HOOKED ON STYLE

A row of hooks or pegs, while maintaining their practical purpose, can be as plain or as colorful as you choose. Wood, cardboard, broken china, and leftover paint can all turn an essential item into a fun addition to your home.

Hanging things on the wall is the perfect storage solution for items that you need to keep close at hand, whether it's a child's favorite jumper or toy or your smallest saucepan. But you can turn a functional set of hooks into an individual and decorative accessory with very little time and effort. Often a dab of paint can be enough: paint a plain wooden backboard in black and then use a selection of gold, silver, and bronze metallic paints to add a gleam to the knobs; or replace wooden knobs with flashy glass ones and cover the board in pink velvet for Fifties glitz.

Cutout shapes in plywood or even cardboard can add an element of fun to a child's room. You can mount them along the top of a backboard or space them between the knobs. For a more grown-up look, use decorative moldings from home furnishing stores, paint with two colors of emulsion, and rub off the second layer of paint to create a distressed effect.

Capitalize on a disaster and use broken china to transform a plain coat rack by pressing fragments into a coating of plaster of paris. Or use mosaic tiles in glittering glass or subtle terracotta to create your own swirly design.

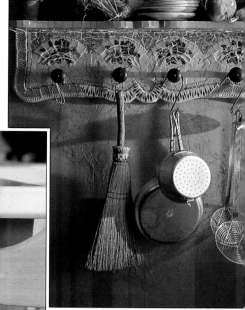

▲ This wall unit, with its rustic mosaic of china tea roses, will bring true naive charm to a country-style kitchen. Smash some chipped plates and then reassemble them in a decorative design on a ready-made unit, or make your own base from cut plywood shapes and wooden pegs.

▲ You can never have too many hooks in a kitchen, and with these wire heart hooks you can have as many as you like – they are made from twisted coat hangers. They have a distinctive Scandinavian air, and their simple design makes them suitable for many different settings.

▶ A basic plywood shape provides an unusual nautical theme for this clever pair of pegs that would be perfect for any child's room. The sails are cut from complementary scraps of fabric, fixed with ribbon and bits of cane. One of the sails even has a little patch on it for a more authentic look.

SHELF LIFE

Make use of sleek shelving to store household clutter
neatly and to create a stylish showcase for your favorite ornaments.
You can make the shelving itself into a smart feature with
decorative brackets and colorful paint effects.

Smart shelving serves two purposes in the home: it creates an attractive and interesting display, and it also provides useful, easy-access storage. Shelves of well-thumbed books in the study or living room, a kitchen hutch stacked with colorful crockery, or glass bathroom shelves bearing perfumes and creams will all add character and a comfortable, lived-in feel to your home.

Individual display shelves and elegant shelf units are ideal for showing off treasured ornaments, leafy potted plants, and framed photographs. A display shelf supported by ornate brackets will create an attractive focal point on a bare wall, and a handsome corner shelf unit will bring a dull corner to life. Try fixing glass shelves in a well-lit alcove or across the front of a window to create a magnificent showcase for ceramics and glassware.

If you like a country-style decor, fix a narrow shelf around the room at picture rail height and use it to display plates and jugs. A shelf above a door or window will create an impression of height; look in furnishing and home supply shops for chunky, wooden curtain poles with shelves attached.

▶ *Natural wicker shelves provide airy and attractive storage for bed linen, clothes, towels, and table linen. These shelves have been fitted into a narrow alcove, making clever use of an awkward space.*

◀ *Transform a plain window by fitting glass shelves into the recess. The shelves will be barely visible and won't block out any light. This is a particularly good spot to display shiny metallic ornaments, like the brass vase, birds, and clock, since they'll reflect the sunlight.*

▼ *For stylish storage on a budget, build up a stack of shelves by laying lightweight planks across filing boxes. These planks and boxes have been painted in fresh shades of green for a bright and cheerful finish. The drawers of the filing boxes provide useful extra storage.*

◄ Scalloped wooden shelf edgings give this bedroom shelf unit a soft and pretty finish. The edgings are made from shaped pieces of board painted to match the shelves, then glued onto the front and sides. If you prefer, you can use brightly colored felt instead of board.

SHELF CHOICE

Shelving can be freestanding, as in bookcases and hutches, or it can be wall-mounted on brackets or supports. Freestanding shelving provides instant storage space and it can be moved around as necessary. It does, however, take up valuable floor space, so in small rooms it's best to choose wall-mounted shelving.

Wooden shelving is most versatile: you can stain or paint it to suit any setting and dress it up with decorative brackets in carved wood or wrought iron. If the shelf will only need to bear a light load, you can even hold it up with ornate plaster corbels. Metal shelving is an excellent choice for the kitchen, since it's easy to keep clean and blends with the functional style of the room. Use elegant glass shelving in alcoves and bathrooms, where it will look sleek and clean.

If you need shelves for heavy items like books, opt for a sturdy material such as wood, or human-made board, or metal, and use strong brackets. Adjustable shelving, which is fitted onto slotted vertical tracks, is especially useful, since you can alter the height of the shelves as necessary. Finish it with a decorative paint effect so it blends with the setting.

▶ A set of five small, semicircular shelves, each bearing a bright plant or ornament, creates an eye-catching display set against this plain green wall. The shelves and brackets are painted vibrant, glossy colors, so they become as much a part of the display as the ornaments.

◄ These cheerful, painted shelves brighten up a dull corner of a bedroom and provide a neat storage spot for shoes. To create a little more space by the door, the three bottom shelves are held up at an angle by sturdy metal hooks fixed to the wall.

If you want to copy this space-saving idea, you'll need to hinge the back edge of each shelf onto a wall-mounted support. Paint the support to match the shelf before you fix it in place.

▼ Elegant, white-painted shelving smartens up the dark area under this stairway and puts an awkwardly shaped space to good use. The shelving is supported by elegant wooden brackets and shaped to fit snugly around the wall on the outer corner of the recess. Note how the baseboard has been used to give the bottom shelf a neat, built-in finish.

DECOUPAGE DELIGHTS

Découpage is the art of decorating with paper scraps: just glue the scraps in place and protect them with glossy coats of varnish. You can use découpage to add a colorful, personal touch to your furniture and home accessories.

Découpage is French for "cutting up," but it's also the name for the increasingly popular pastime of decorating a surface with scraps of paper. It's a very simple craft and an easy and economical way to give a new look to all kinds of furniture and accessories.

Anything goes in découpage: you can cover a whole cupboard or screen with myriad colorful scraps, or just add a dainty border of images, or a single exquisite motif. You can découpage any reasonably firm surface; make sure it can be dampened without buckling or warping, since it will come in contact with wet glue and varnish. Suitable surfaces include wood, glass, metal, and plastic. The protective coats of varnish mean your découpage will stand up well to everyday wear and tear, even on areas like tabletops and tray surfaces.

CHOOSING PAPER SCRAPS

You can use all kinds of paper scraps for découpage. Traditional favorites are images of flowers, fruits, birds, and butterflies, cut from greeting cards, wrapping paper, wallpaper, old books, and glossy magazines. You can also choose abstract motifs cut from the same sources. Alternatively, you can recycle scraps, such as ornate labels from jars and bottles, decorative paper packaging, old stamps, or even photocopies for a monochromatic finish.

For the best results, choose motifs with clear outlines. The paper should be of reasonably good quality, and if you're mixing motifs, these should all be of roughly the same thickness.

Some craft shops and suppliers sell sheets of motifs specially designed for

▼ *Brighten up a battered metal watering can by covering it with floral découpage. Look for pictures of colorful flowers in old gardening magazines and books, on seed packets, and on greeting cards.*

▲ *Dainty pansies, cut from gift wrap, make an exquisite border for this papier-mâché plate and look pretty on the matching blue egg. Several coats of varnish provide a protective, glossy finish.*

découpage. There's a good range of Victorian-style images, since the Victorians loved découpage – these are great for creating an antique look.

DÉCOUPAGE THEMES

If you're looking for inspiration for your découpage, choose a theme: let the object you're decorating dictate the style. You could decorate a watering can with floral paper scraps, a drinks tray with labels from liqueur bottles, or a toilette box with pretty soap and perfume labels.

Alternatively, just choose a theme that you're especially fond of and one that's full of colorful images. Flowers are a popular choice, or you could choose animals, seaside images, or even eye-catching insects like butterflies, dragonflies, and ladybugs.

Personal themes are also fun; base your découpage on your family or an enjoyable holiday. For the latter, take images from photographs, brochures, and postcards and use them to découpage a box of holiday souvenirs.

▲ *Make a clever container for your stationery by covering a plain wooden box with used stamps. Strip off any old paint or varnish and seal the surface before you begin.*

▼ *Oriental fans, cheeky cherubs, and romantic pastoral scenes were all great favorites with Victorian découpage enthusiasts. Use them to decorate a range of accessories.*

▲ Découpage a plain tray with a garland of exquisite floral motifs or with a single large bloom. Before you begin, paint the tray white or pale primrose yellow for a fresh background, or black for a sophisticated look.

▲ This elegantly découpaged table previously painted black is topped with several coats of varnish, giving it a satin-smooth, glossy finish. The varnish also protects the table against everyday wear and tear. This is an excellent way to imitate expensive, lacquered furniture from the Orient, for a fraction of the price.

◄ Columns of newspaper print cover the base of this lamp, giving it a stylish finish that's ideal for a modern setting. For a softer, more personal variation, you could substitute handwritten sheets of paper for the newspaper. Or re-create the black-and-white effect in a more sophisticated style, using photocopies of old prints – classical motifs, such as Greek or Roman columns and statues, are perfect.

~3~

COLOR SCHEMES
FOR YOUR HOME

WARM & COOL COLORS

The mood of any room depends largely on the color scheme. Walls, window dressings, furniture, and carpets will all affect the finished atmosphere and create a cool, spacious look or a cozy, intimate one.

◄ *Icy blue walls and pale soft furnishings will create a bedroom that is a cool and tranquil retreat. A white cotton bedspread adds a fresh touch, while the blue chair provides color interest.*

The secret of any good interior design lies in the use of color. As a general rule, colors can be grouped as warm or cool. Warm colors look cheerful and, logically, evoke a feeling of warmth and coziness, while cool colors create a sense of spaciousness and tranquility.

WARM ROOMS

Warm colors are reds, pinks, oranges, and yellows, the colors associated with sunshine and firelight. They range from hot colors, such as rich red, golden yellow, spicy orange, and russet to softer warm shades like primrose, peach, pink, and beige, and white tinted with any of the warm colors.

Yellow is the most cheering of all the colors; it has actually been shown to make people feel happier, perhaps because it reminds us of summer sunshine. Rich shades like buttercup and

◀ *This unusual bedroom is part of a converted warehouse. Despite the austerity of the girder in the ceiling and the industrial window, the room is given a coziness with its soft, parchment-colored walls and cream and red furnishings.*

yellow ocher are the most warming; cooler shades, such as lemon yellow and greenish yellow will look cold in comparison.

Warm colors appear to advance toward you, making large rooms seem more intimate. The hotter the color, the more the walls seem to advance, but unless you are confident with color, it is best to avoid very strong colors, which can be overpowering. Choose earthy or muted shades instead, the colors of natural clays, firelight, or dried flowers.

Colors can also psychologically affect the temperature. Terra-cotta and rosy pink feel cozy and warm, even on a cold day. This makes them ideal for gloomy, north-facing rooms, which can otherwise look bleak and uninviting. Add some well-stuffed sofas, rugs, lamps, and other comfortable touches to complete the welcoming look.

◄ The opulence of the East is conjured up in this wonderfully decadent room with its exotic furnishings. Burnt orange dominates to create a warm and sultry effect.

▲ Deep yellow wallpaper combines with pale lemon cupboards and golden yellow curtains to make this room warm and bright. Brass fittings and ornaments add a gleaming finishing touch.

▲ Use a combination of colors and furnishings to warm up a large bathroom. The wall color is echoed in the curtain frills, cushions, roses, and picture.

▶ Rich terra-cotta walls create an intimate dining area. This is a particularly good choice of color for a dining room, since reds and terra-cottas are said to stimulate the appetite.

COOL ROOMS

Cool colors can make a room seem more restful and spacious. They are colors that remind us of the sea and sky: blues, greens, gray, some of the bluer purples, white, and white with a hint of the cool colors.

The restful qualities of cool colors make them a good choice for bathrooms and bedrooms, where you'll want to unwind. The easiest and most popular shades of blue and green are those that have been tempered with a warm color, making them softer and more muted. These colors include soft turquoise, sky blue, sage, olive, and pale avocado.

Cool colors create space because they seem to push walls and ceilings back. This makes them a good choice for small rooms, but because they can also make a room seem colder, they should be used with care.

For small, north-facing rooms, temper the cooling effect of blue or green walls with touches of warmer colors. For example, choose deep apricot or yellow curtains, which will let a flood of warm light into the room. Alternatively, add room accessories in warm shades to make a cool scheme more friendly: cushions, a throw, or rugs in shades such as apricot, terra-cotta, or yellow add a welcome touch.

▲ This Victorian-style bathroom makes a bold use of color. An intense, powdery shade of blue is applied to the walls and the exterior of an old ball-and-claw bath. Ivory linen is cleverly used to disguise the basin's plumbing and makes an unusual shower curtain.

▲ The coolest of greens and creams combine in an elegant drawing room. Since the room is filled with light from the large window, it can afford this cool treatment. The rug and china also add a touch of warmth.

▶ A lovely mixture of cool shades creates a tranquil and refined bedroom. Pale gray-green stripes in the wallpaper are echoed in the deeper green of the glazed cotton curtains. The bed and tablecloth pick up the gray tinge, but use a bluer color set on white. White in the lamps, bedstead, and paintwork draws all the elements together.

SUNBURST YELLOW

Bring sunshine into your home with a splash of yellow
paint and some matching fittings and accessories.
It's a wonderfully warm and cheering color that will brighten
up dark areas and add zest to plain rooms.

Color can make a strong impact on your home. Yellow's cheerful springlike tones are particularly potent, varying from soft to strong, and they help to brighten up your home – and you.

Yellow's strength comes from the fact that it is a simple primary color. Yet, at the same time it's a difficult color to define. The yellow spectrum is broad. It ranges from orangey and golden tones at the red end of the spectrum to acidic lemon yellow at the green end. Because of this, it can be tricky to make different yellows work together in close proximity. Lemon yellow would not work well in the same room with mustard, for example.

CHOOSING A SHADE

It's possible to paint every room of your home in a different shade of yellow, since the spectrum is so varied. Sunlight yellow is a great color for brightening up a dark room or a hallway. A narrow and gloomy passageway will be transformed if it is simply given a welcoming coat of yellow. Try using yellow in a room that catches the morning light – sunlight pouring into a yellow room has a wonderful, glowing quality.

Lemon is a youthful shade, and it goes very well in a child's bedroom, particularly when you combine it with a patterned blind or a bright and fun wallpaper border.

▶ *Light on the yellow walls brings the sunshine indoors. The curtains and cushion, which harmonize with the chair fabric and diamond patchwork quilt, show how subtle coordination can make a quiet corner both attractive and inviting.*

▲*Yellow walls contrast brilliantly with the colorful cupboard, the vivid ceramics, and the bright window blind. The splashback behind the sink provides a clever link between the yellow walls and the wooden surfaces.*

▶ *Rays of early morning sunshine pour through a big sash window, lighting up a corner of this comfortable family kitchen. The pale, understated yellow of the corner cupboard reflects the yellow in the curtain fabric and the grapes stenciled on the wall. The yellows are balanced with touches of fresh green in the curtains and the stenciled leaves, giving a look that is warm, fresh, and inviting.*

Children's rooms are one of the few areas of the home where it works to combine yellow with another primary color. Try using red with yellow for a bold, happy scheme.

Yellow used with green and white creates a fresh, lively look for a living room or bedroom. Another pleasing but softer combination is primrose and gray. Mixing warm and cool colors will create an interesting, harmonious scheme anywhere in your home.

For instance, try a daffodil yellow with touches of sky blue to bring springlike freshness into any room.

YELLOW AND WOOD

Certain woods, like bleached pine, can clash with strong yellow tones. Yellow looks better with antique pines, ash (which has a grayish tinge), or dark woods like mahogany.

▲ *Bright yellow curtains form the strong accent in this sedate, cool sitting room. This vibrant color is picked up in the patterned recliner.*

◀ *There is an infinite variety of yellow flowers that bloom throughout the year. These creamy yellow roses bring a breath of summer, and their full-blown petals highlight the floral wall frieze.*

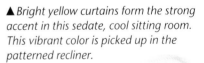

◀ Yellow gingham curtains adorn tall patio doors in the house where the French painter Monet used to live. The diverse range of colors in the room, including the rich aqua doors, ensure that the yellow ceiling and walls are not overwhelming.

▼ Broad yellow stripes provide the perfect background for this lavish bed and novel wallpaper border. The confident stripes frame the bed and help visually to reduce the height of the ceiling.

▼ Fresh, clear yellow stripes are accentuated by the golden wood of the bed and complemented by the floral wallpaper stripes.

GOING GREEN

Bring the great outdoors into your home with fresh and
invigorating shades of green. Choose from pale shades of
apple through lush, tropical greens to bright, citrus
greens. You'll find nature's palette is wonderfully varied.

G reen is the prime color of nature, which is why it is
so wonderfully easy to live with in the home. It can
be refreshing and invigorating, or soothing and
relaxing. Use it for your whole color scheme or add just a
touch of green with furnishings and accessories.

WARM AND COOL GREENS

If you want to introduce quite a lot of green into your
home, think about whether you want it to have a cooling or
a warming effect. Cool greens are those that have a blue
tinge, like the blue-greens of the sea, of peppermint, duck
eggs, and spruce. Use them in rooms that receive plenty of
sunlight for a calm and refreshing ambience. Warm greens
have hints of yellow in them and include the yellow-greens
of leafy shoots, of limes, lettuces, and young green apples.
They're great for warming up cool rooms and injecting
them with the vitality of spring.

When you're choosing furnishings, always consider the
colors that will surround them in the room – take samples

◄ *The warm, muted greens of these patterned fabrics make
them a relaxing choice for a living or dining room. A vase of
yellow flowers provides a fresh accent color.*

▼ *Green furniture adds interest to the neutral scheme of
this kitchen. The pine tabletop, terra-cotta pots, and red
geraniums all warm up the room and counterbalance the
cool green paintwork.*

▼ *Fiery red tulips teamed with an apple-
green vase make a bold display. Red
and green is a vibrant color combination
– use it to add vitality to your home.*

of these colors with you to the store if you can. If the room has mainly warm colors in it, a cool green will add a touch of freshness, while a warm green will make it really cozy. If it has mainly cool shades, a blue-green may cool it down too much; it would be better to balance it with a warm yellow-green, like pea green.

CHOOSING FABRICS AND ACCESSORIES

Patterned fabrics and wallpaper with plenty of green in them are particularly attractive. Look for colorful floral and leafy prints, which will give your home lots of fresh country charm. These prints are a useful starting point for a color scheme.

Sometimes, just a few green accessories are enough to freshen up a room. As well as cushions, lamps, and ornaments, you can add some natural splashes of green in the form of leafy potted plants or a basket brimming with green apples, pears, limes, and grapes.

▶ *Sea-green is a striking and appropriate color choice for the walls of an attic bathroom. The bright pink of the wicker chair, bath, and towels creates a bold contrast; and together with the dark wood furnishings, it gives an otherwise cool room a warm and cozy feel.*

▼ *White and green is a fresh and elegant color combination, ideal for this handsome living room. The lime green of the walls evokes spring freshness, but its sharpness is softened by the color-washed paint effect.*

▲ *A collection of green china makes an attractive display on a kitchen hutch. Here, all the crockery has a cabbage-leaf pattern, but you could create a similar effect using green china in a mixture of designs.*

▲ *Shades of olive green infuse this bedroom with a calm and relaxing atmosphere. By using differently patterned fabrics in the same shade of green, and staining the wooden furniture to match, an interesting scheme is created. The white flowers, lampshade and bed linen provide a subtle accent.*

◄ *A colorful floral fabric or wallpaper with plenty of foliage in the design is an attractive way to introduce green into your home. Here, a bold floral pattern is teamed with green striped wallpaper, green paintwork, and green furniture. Even the wicker armchair is painted to match. The effect is fresh and summery.*

ACCENT ON RED

Red is vibrant and exciting, daring and bold, and yet comfortingly
warm and welcoming. An all-over red room scheme can
be hard to live with, but you'll find small touches of red or red
mixed with other colors friendly and invigorating.

▲ *A modern two-seater sofa covered in vibrant red cotton makes an eye-catching focal point in this living room. The earthy, natural tones of bare wood and wicker provide the perfect setting for the rich red fabric.*

▼ *Warm red accents provided by the cushions, throw, fruit bowl, and ethnic rugs raise the temperature of this cool room and create a balanced effect. The brick flooring provides a complementary background for the red accents.*

For color schemes that look flat or dull, or for rooms that are cold and sterile, a dashing splash of red is the perfect remedy. A bowl of ripe red apples or a vase of scarlet blooms will instantly raise the temperature of a cool blue or green room. Or use lively red furnishings, such as cushions, lampshades, and rugs, to create fiery focal points within a plain or neutral scheme.

ACCENT IDEAS

There are all sorts of ways to introduce lively splashes of red into your home. You can make a bold statement by using red in large quantities: upholster your sofa or armchairs in bright red cotton chintz, cover your bed with a cheerful red quilt or duvet cover, or hang your windows with sumptuous red velvet drapes.

Alternatively, choose a lower-key but equally stimulating look by adding smaller red accessories to your home. These can be soft furnishings, such as cushions, rugs, tablecloths, and picture bows, or ornaments such as painted crockery or ruby-red glassware. Or you can opt for some eye-catching red paintwork on baseboards, window frames, or wooden chairs – you could paint them solid red or add a dainty red stencil. And don't forget

all the red accents that nature has to offer: a bowl of red fruits, a vase of red blooms, or a cluster of winter berries makes an invigorating display.

RED WITH…

You can use red accents to enhance rooms of more or less any color and decorative style. In cozy, cottage-style homes and informal kitchens, opt for hot reds and cheerful red patterned fabrics like red-and-white gingham or polka-dot designs. In more formal rooms, use the deep reds that were so popular with the Victorians – these look sophisticated and dramatic, as well as warm and inviting. Keep an eye open for red-based tartans and paisley prints in rich shades of red.

Red and green is a fresh combination, and one of nature's favorites. Use warm red accents to counterbalance the coolness of a green room; and use red on your deck or patio, with red cushions on outdoor furniture and red table linen for al fresco meals.

You'll also find red makes a fabulous foil for natural woods, whether light or dark. Stencil red designs onto pine chests and kitchen cupboards to enhance their fresh, country cottage appeal. Or upholster a mahogany chair with some rich red fabric to give it a handsome and comfortable finish.

▲ Splashes of red decorate the walls, floor, and furnishings for a look that's energetic yet cozy. The red stenciling on the chest and the red chair webbing are set off by their backgrounds of warm pine.

▼A deep, sophisticated shade of red is the perfect accent color for this formal bathroom, where it's used for wall borders and curtain trims. A rich red picture bow and hanging plates enhance the look.

▼ Red-handled cutlery and a vivid red napkin are teamed with red-painted crockery, all laid out on a natural pine tray, for a cheerful start to the day.

► Smart red-and-white checked fabrics, like this large-check tablecloth, feel cozy and homey as well as fresh and lively. Here, red dining chairs lift the red of the fabric and create a coordinated effect. A bowl of ripe nectarines adds a subtler hint of red.

▲ Make use of red accessories to invigorate your patio or deck. Here, plain and patterned red fabrics are combined to create a striking tablecloth and matching cushion.

► Lots of different patterns are combined in this enchanting red-accented bedroom. Large and small red-and-white checks are used on the headboard, bedcover, and armchair, while red-based florals cover the walls, curtains, bed skirt, and pillow. If you want to combine different patterns like this, use shades of red that are very similar to each other.

PRETTY PASTELS

Let soft pastels give your home a fresh and airy feel. Use them to create restful bedrooms and nurseries, sleek bathrooms and kitchens, and elegant dining and living rooms. You'll find pastels very versatile and a delight to live with.

Pastels are soft, chalky shades, created by mixing white with other colors. For example, red mixed with white creates pale pink, blue and white make powdery blue.

Depending on how much white they contain, some pastels are far paler than others. Use pale pastels as background colors to create restful schemes. You'll find they mix well with other colors and can be spiced up with bold accessories. Strong pastels are ideal for discreet but colorful accents in neutral and pale pastel schemes.

PASTEL OPTIONS

You can use pastels in your home to create many different looks. Team large areas of flat pastel color with touches of pure white for a crisp, sleek look that's perfect for modern bathrooms and kitchens. If you prefer pretty, feminine schemes, introduce pastel print fabrics and wallpapers into your home, such as floral designs, candy stripes, and pastel polka-dot sheers. For elegant living and dining rooms, team powdery pastels with rich cream and add gilt detailing to furniture and to picture and mirror frames.

◀ For schemes bursting with color, mix several different pastels; you'll find they sit well together. Balance the pastels with warm, earthy shades, like terra-cotta, umber, or ocher. In this room, the classic pastel shades of the picture frames and the harlequin floor – Wedgwood blue, pale pink, pistachio, and primrose – are warmed up by touches of deep olive green on the floor and a pale umber and buff wall.

▼ Pastels have a fresh, crisp feel, which makes them an excellent choice for a modern kitchen. Here, pale pink, peach, and pistachio have been used on the walls, units, shelves, and even the crockery. Touches of white paintwork freshen up the scheme, while a black-and-white checkered floor adds a dramatic flourish. Natural wooden worktops, gleaming chrome accessories and a pair of paint-splattered black and pistachio chairs make striking accents that help to lift the color scheme.

PASTELS PLUS

A predominantly pastel scheme can look sterile, so it's a good idea to warm it up with some rich, earthy shades. Try Wedgwood blue teamed with golden ocher, pale pink with rich olive green, or pistachio with rosy grape.

Introducing natural wood furniture and accessories into a pastel scheme will also make it warmer and friendlier. Choose honey-colored varieties, such as oak, old pine, or birch, rather than bleached or dark woods. Natural cane furniture is also an excellent foil for pastels.

For a dramatic flourish, team soft pastels with glinting metallic accents. In the kitchen below left, shiny chrome accessories, like the toaster and coffee pot, lift the pastel scheme and give it a sleek, modern feel. In a more traditional kitchen, you could display pewter plates, brass or tinware instead. Try enhancing a pastel dining room with gilt detailing on mirror and picture frames, or with gleaming silver trays and candlesticks. Or team smart Venetian blinds in coordinating colors, as in the bedroom on page 102.

▲ *Pastels needn't always be used as background colors; in a neutral scheme, you can use strong pastels to create subtle accents, which will add interest without being over-powering. This charming set of floral cushions, in strong pastel shades of yellow, blue, and pink, gives a lift to the pale gray-blue sofa and the matching drapes behind.*

◄ *In this grand bedroom, powdery pastels are teamed with handsome furniture and fine gilding to create an airy and elegant scheme, which has its roots in eighteenth-century rococo style.*

◀ *Create a stunning outdoor display with strong pastels in aqua, pink, and turquoise. Here, these colors have been used to paint geranium-filled hanging plant pots for a fresh, Mediterranean feel.*

▼ *Pastel shades look wonderfully dramatic teamed with black, as you can see from these cups and saucers. This striking color combination is typical of Art Deco style.*

▼*Try mixing strong and pale pastels to create a colorful, yet restful scheme. In this bedroom, the colors range from the pale gray of the walls and carpet to the medium tones of the Venetian blinds and the strong pink and blue of the cushions.*

HOT TERRA-COTTA

Spice up your home with the warm, earthy shades of terra-cotta.
Use palest, pink-tinged terra-cotta to lend a soft touch to
walls, floors, and upholstery, or opt for hot red terra-cotta accents
to add vibrancy to cool or neutral schemes.

Terra-cotta is an Italian word meaning "baked earth" – it's the color of Mediterranean-style terra-cotta pots that are made from clay and baked in an oven. It's a wonderfully soft, warm color that comes in many different shades, from palest, pinky-brown corals and ochers to rich russet-brown and vibrant brick-red.

SHADES OF TERRA-COTTA

The soft, pale shades of terra-cotta are warm and restful. Use them on large areas, such as walls, floors, and upholstery, where they'll provide an excellent background for soft or bright colors. Blend them with other warm pastels, such as pale pink, yellow, and cream, for a relaxing ambience, or use them to counterbalance strong, bold colors, like bright blue, aqua, and fuchsia, for a scheme with a distinctly Mediterranean feel.

Deep, rich shades of terra-cotta are vibrant and exciting, without being harsh or garish. If you want to make an impact, use these colors to cover large areas of a room: for example, use orange-brown terra-cotta tiles on the floor or brick-red gloss paint on the walls. Alternatively, use rich terra-cottas as accent colors on cushions, tiebacks, rugs, throws, and lampshades; they're ideal for warming up a cool room scheme and can easily spice up a neutral-colored setting.

TERRA-COTTA FABRICS

You'll find lots of terra-cotta fabrics in the stores, from plain cottons, striped ticking, and contemporary checks, to elaborate kilim designs and ethnic prints. Keep an eye open for hand-printed, ethnic-style fabrics, and rugs and hangings from the Middle East – many textiles like these are colored with natural dyes in beautifully rich, strong shades of terra-cotta.

▼ Terra-cotta looks great with other earthy shades. Team terra-cotta pots and tiles with the natural dye colors of a kilim for an exotic look.

▲ This cozy den gets its warmth from the natural colors of the kilim cushions and ethnic throw. Terra-cotta shades and bold patterns stand out against the plain, pale furniture, walls, and varnished floorboards.

◄ The walls of this sun room were painted cream, then rubbed over with pink-tinged terra-cotta to create a warm backdrop for the plants. Window frames painted in a hot shade of terra-cotta give the room a lift.

▲ Practical orange-red terra-cotta floor tiles are teamed with gray slate insets in this classic hot and cold color combination.

▶ Masks and symbols cover the bold fabric on this armchair. The terra-cotta in the print is picked up by a spicy, terra-cotta cord, tied across the front of the chair to secure the fabric.

▶ *Hot terra-cotta works well with cool blue: in this bedroom, splashes of terra-cotta in the bed linen, curtains, and paintwork take on an even greater warmth and intensity against the bright blue background of the walls and sheets.*

▼ *Terra-cotta tiles look warm and inviting on kitchen walls and floors. Their glowing tones complement natural wood cupboards and fittings, and you'll find their charm increases even more with age. Here, terra-cotta wall tiles make a practical and stylish splashback. On the bottom two rows, they're interspersed with cool, gray slate tiles to create a checkered border.*

▼ *These exotic cushions are made from Indian-style fabrics in rich shades of terra-cotta and trimmed with twisted cords in complementary colors.*

BLACK AND WHITE

Use black and white in your home to produce chic detailing
and dramatic effects. It's a powerful combination you
can use to create a sleek, modern interior, or one with a
classically elegant feel.

Black and white is one of the most striking color combinations that you can use in your home. Its impact comes from the fact that black and white are complete opposites, presenting the strongest possible contrast to the eye. This means that in a black and white scheme, there's no blurring of colors and lines – all details stand out and demand attention.

BLACK AND WHITE ROOMS

A whole scheme based purely on black and white can look stunning, but you'll find it works better in some rooms than in others. For the scheme to look crisp and chic, the room needs to be kept free of clutter: a formal dining room is more suitable for a black and white scheme than a busy family room. In a bedroom, black and white can look somewhat sterile and cool, whereas in a kitchen or bathroom it can create a welcome atmosphere of order and cleanliness.

You can make a black and white room scheme instantly warmer and friendlier by using an accent color to provide some visual relief. A strong color, such as bright red, blue, or yellow, works well, as do metallics such as gold and bronze.

USING BLACK AND WHITE

The most successful black and white room schemes contain an interesting mix of patterns and plains. Black and white patterned wallpaper and fabrics are classic favorites, and you'll always find a good range in furnishing stores. Try to mix simple, geometric designs, such as stripes, checks, and dots, with softer, less structured patterns, such as mini-print florals or toiles de Jouy, to create a balanced effect.

Stain floorboards a glossy black, or lime them to create a textured effect. Alternatively, use floor tiles in one

▲ One of the pleasures of creating a black and white room scheme is the ease with which you can mix different patterns. The black and white check on these cupboard doors complements the elaborate design of the wallpaper.

▶ Black and white crockery always looks chic and won't date. Collect a matching set or a mix of designs.

▶ In this modern, streamlined kitchen, white is the dominant color on the walls and tiled marble floor, with the small black tiles providing strong accents. Note how well the pale gray storage units work in this scheme, uniting the two extremes of black and white.

color or in a dramatic black and white checkerboard design. If you prefer carpets, choose a mottled black and white pattern rather than plain white or black, which can be hard to keep clean.

Black and white walls and floors make a striking backdrop for many different styles of furniture. Modern furniture in stained wood, chrome, leather, or plastic will look sleek and crisp, while natural, dark, and light wood furniture will warm up the room for a friendlier look.

Black and white makes a dramatic two-color accent, especially in rooms with strong color schemes. Add black and white striped cushions to a red sofa, or hang a black and white blind in a bright yellow kitchen.

▶ *White walls, hung with black and white prints, are a natural foil for the clean, sleek lines of a modern dining table and chairs. A vase of white lilies repeats the color theme but has a softening effect. Natural wood floorboards add a warm accent.*

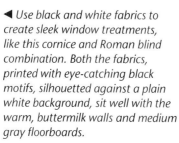

▲ A bright red quilt and a stack of red books warm up this black and white bedroom. The room combines sleek, modern furniture and boldly patterned bed linen with some comfortingly traditional features, such as a checkerboard floor and framed copies of old black-and-white photographs. The neat, symmetrical arrangement of the furniture and accessories helps to give the scheme added crispness.

◄ Use black and white fabrics to create sleek window treatments, like this cornice and Roman blind combination. Both the fabrics, printed with eye-catching black motifs, silhouetted against a plain white background, sit well with the warm, buttermilk walls and medium gray floorboards.

▲ Black and white trimmings, such as braid, fringing, and piping, will add chic detailing to all kinds of accessories. Here, they've been used to pep up a plain green lampshade – the trims are glued in place around the edges of the shade and at intervals down the sides.

~4~

USING PATTERN
IN THE HOME

MINI-MAGIC

The dainty pattern of a mini-print has a charm all its own.
Use mini-prints to adorn anything from walls to
washstands, and combine them with other favorite designs.
For versatility, you'll find mini-prints hard to beat.

Mini-prints are small repeating patterns that are made up of tiny motifs on a plain background. The motifs can be anything from delicate flowers to bold geometric forms, like spots or the intricate shapes found on Provençal mini-prints. The choice is almost endless.

It is possible to buy a whole range of home furnishing items printed with exquisite mini-print designs. They are to be found on wallpaper, fabrics, carpets, and tiles, as well as on accessories like lampshades, bed linen, towels, and even crockery.

PERFECT COMBINATIONS

Because they're so small and dainty, mini-prints can be used in abundance in a room without being overpowering. You can also successfully combine them with many other patterns, such as large florals and stripes. Lots of manufacturers now design coordinated fabric and wallpaper ranges, in which mini-prints are mixed and matched with many other colors and patterns to give stylish, easy-to-use combinations.

If you want to build up your own pattern combinations, one of the best ways to achieve a unified effect is to keep to one family of colors, such as blues or pinks. You can balance out the overall look and stop it from becoming too busy by adding some plain accessories, such as lampshades, cushions, and curtain tiebacks.

NOW YOU SEE IT…

Mini-print motifs are often so small and closely spaced that the pattern "reads" as a single color when you step back from it. This is because from a distance the tiny motifs all seem to merge together.

◄ *Keeping to a limited range of colors when building up your own combination of mini-prints will create a unified effect. In these life-sized samples, the main colors are pink, white, and green.*

▼ *Mini-prints are a popular choice for small bathrooms. Here, blue and white mini-print wallpaper is the perfect background for the floral blind and patterned tiles.*

To give yourself an idea of how a mini-print will look from afar, take a few steps back from it and look at it through half-closed eyes. You should gain a clear impression of the dominant color, which is useful, especially if you're planning to use it over a large area, like a wall or floor.

If you want a mini-print with motifs that stay clearly defined when you look at it from a distance, choose a pattern with widely spaced, strongly colored motifs and a subtle, light colored background.

USING MINI-PRINTS

Mini-prints are so delicate that you can use them in the smallest of rooms. You'll find that they add all the color and interest of a larger print, without being overwhelming. Small bathrooms, bedrooms, and hallways are all perfect candidates for mini-prints.

▼ *There's no such thing as too many mini-prints. The wallpaper and headboard prints are from a coordinated line, and the lampshade, bedspread, and tissue-box covers have been made up from matching mini-print fabrics.*

▲ *A combination of mini-prints, sprigs, large florals, and plains give this bedroom a warm and cozy feel. The simple color scheme prevents the room from being too busy. A plain carpet, lampshade, and bedspread, and sober mahogany furniture, balance the overall effect.*

▼ *An understated yellow and white mini-print provides an elegant backdrop for a display of gilt-edged china.*

To make a small room seem more spacious, team your mini-print with a plain color. This looks fabulous if you use a chair rail to divide the two. Keep to cool, pale shades like pastel blue or lemon, and the roomy effect will be further increased.

One of the main advantages of mini-prints is that they're so easy and practical to use, especially on the walls of irregularly shaped spaces like attic rooms. The small scale of the pattern means it's easy to match neatly across odd angles. The pattern also helps to disguise an uneven wall surface, whereas a plain color or a regular stripe would accentuate the flaw.

▶ The magnificent mini-print designs on these cushions are typical of traditional Provençal fabrics. They have vibrant, contrasting colors and the motifs stand out sharply against the background, even from a distance.

▼ Plain flower pots wrapped with colorful mini-print fabrics make a charming shelf display.

LAY IT ON THE LINE

Stripes have a smart and timeless quality that makes them
suitable for both modern and traditional interiors. And you
can use the almost magical properties of stripes to
make your rooms look taller, broader, smarter, or brighter.

Stripes range from neat
and simple styles, like
those on ticking fabric,
to elegant Regency designs
and the bold and cheerful
stripes of fairground tents.
They mix well with decorative patterns, such as flowers
and foliage, and look stylish
teamed with plain fabrics
and bold checks.

TRICKS WITH STRIPES

The magic of stripes lies in
their versatility: they can be
used in so many different
ways. Stripes can enhance or
restrain the proportions of a
room or a piece of furniture.
Thin, vertical stripes emphasize height rather than width
and can make a room look
taller. Used around a tall
window, narrow stripes will
draw attention to the height
of a window, whereas broad
stripes will have a shortening
and widening effect.

Stripes can also enhance
shapes. When upholstering
a chair or sofa, let the stripes
on the fabric follow the lines
of your furniture. A high-
armed Chesterfield sofa, for
example, will look best if the
striped fabric runs vertically
up and over the arms, and
down the sides of the chair
toward the floor. Because
stripes are linear and direc-
tional, they lend themselves
to rectangular items, too: for
example, running down a
Roman blind or around the
lower edge of a bedcover.

FABRIC STRIPES

Stripes can be either printed
or woven. Woven stripes
can be in the same color, a
contrasting color, or a combination of the two. They
have greater depth of color
than printed stripes.

STRIPES PLUS

Take the trim, businesslike stripe one step further to create a more feminine look by using coordinating florals, or choose combined striped and floral designs. There are many ranges that include plain stripes, stripes with florals, small florals, mini-prints, and plains. A combination of floral and striped designs will create a homey, comfortable, but not overly feminine scheme, with the stripes providing a restraining influence.

Stripes can be formed in unexpected ways: for instance, lines of rosebuds or leaves on wallpaper or fabric will give the impression of stripes without the severity. Or you could introduce the crispness of stripes to a room with potted plants. Many houseplants have leaves or blooms that are distinctly striped. One or even several of these can be used to make an interesting feature in a room.

◄ *Using striped fabric with the stripes in a horizontal direction will help to make a fairly bare and spacious room more intimate.*

▼ *This dining room shows stripes combined with other patterns. The checks and bow print soften the bold lines of the upholstery fabric.*

▼ *If you like stripes but don't want to overdo it, try striped accessories. Vividly striped crockery in bold, primary shades will add a burst of color to your dining table or serve as an attractive display on open shelves.*

PROBLEM STRIPES

If you choose Regency-style wallpaper for a tall room in your home, make sure that the walls aren't too bumpy; any irregularities will distort the stripes and will look unprofessional. Remember, too, that the straight symmetrical lines of stripes will emphasize odd angles.

Try not to allow strong, vertically striped wallpaper to become cluttered. Hang only one or two prints or paintings on the walls and save any lavish decoration for the window treatments. Elaborate, striped curtains will echo the linear theme of striped walls, but you may need to soften the look. Swags and tails emphasize the flow of the fabric and make the stripes come alive.

► *The understated stripes of the wallpaper provide a quiet background for the rich, glowing tones of the wooden chest and floor. The deep blue in the striped chair fabric adds color to this corner of the room.*

▼ *The strong vertical lines of the curtains and screen are broken by a bold lion motif. The subtle red on red striped wallpaper echoes the striped theme without letting it become overly dominant.*

▼*Stripes do not have to be formed by a solid line. The rows of trailing ivy on this curtain give the distinct impression of stripes and do the same work – they lead the eye up, adding height to the room.*

▲ *Plants such as these crocuses reflect a striped theme and will add a touch of color.*

▶ *The recessed shelves are covered in the same wallpaper as the rest of the bathroom, leaving the lines unbroken around the room.*

◀ *Patterns that combine stripes with florals are very effective. The pretty stripes of the pillow and wallpaper are repeated in bands on the complementary print used for the bedcover and curtains, and although the stripes run in different directions, the consistent theme of blue, pink, and yellow provides a link.*

▼ *Stripes of different widths look good together. The border tile repeats the striped theme, but its pattern adds a new dimension.*

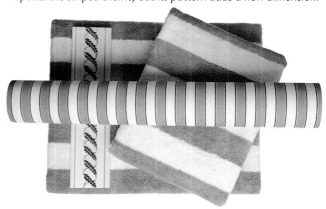

CHECK IT OUT

Simple checks combining two or three colors look crisp and fresh, and their straightforward designs fit easily into any setting. They're a delight to use in the home, where you can mix and match them with all sorts of other patterns.

Checks range from the simple to the elaborate and come in a huge variety of color combinations. Simple checks, like gingham, have a gridlike pattern of evenly spaced lines, usually in two or three colors. More elaborate checks, like madras and tartan, have three or more colors that cross over in a complex grid of irregularly spaced lines and merge to form yet more colors.

Simple checks are the easiest to use in the home. They have a clean, fresh look that complements any room, whatever its style or function. Checks in classic, muted colors look elegant in a sophisticated den or hallway, for example, while those in bright, clear colors add fun and warmth to a kitchen. Light, cheery checks are ideal for bathrooms and cottage-style dining rooms, while checks in quiet colors suit the calm mood of a study or work area. The simplicity of checks gives them child appeal, so they're also an excellent choice for the nursery or playroom.

▶ *Make mealtimes more colorful with cheerful checked crockery – great for creating a cozy, cottage feel, especially in kitchens.*

▼ *Crisp checks and soft florals work well together in this airy bedroom. The fabrics, which are from a coordinated line, have been imaginatively combined: for example, small check borders cut from the floral fabric create a pretty stand-up heading and rosette tiebacks for the curtains.*

USING SIMPLE CHECKS

Checks never go out of fashion, so checked fabrics, wallpapers, and accessories are always available in the stores. Take a tip from interior designers and mix checks with plains and patterns. You'll find checks included in many coordinated fabric lines alongside stripes, plains, and florals.

If you're planning a color scheme from scratch, a checked fabric can be an inspiring starting point. For example, you could team a lively blue, yellow, and white check with cool, blue color-washed walls, crisp white paintwork, and sunny yellow accents.

Use checks to give an instant lift to a plain scheme, especially if you want to retain a crisp and uncluttered look. Watch for checked accessories, such as crockery or bed and table linen; scatter checked cushions across a plain sofa, hang pretty gingham curtains in an overly stark kitchen, or lay a checked rug over a neutral carpet.

For a lively look, mix simple checks in different colors and sizes. You could make curtains from a large check, and trim them with piping, a frill, and tiebacks in a small check.

It's fun to create your own checked effects. Make a checked splashback in a kitchen or bathroom with tiles in two colors, or stitch a simple checked patchwork cushion or bedspread. You can even paint your own set of checked crockery.

▲ Checks are a hit with all age groups. In this child's room, bold checks in deep, forest green cover the walls and soft furnishings to create a lively and stimulating decor. Bright red accents and doggy motifs lighten the effect.

◄ Two-color checks always complement each other, even when you combine unlikely colors. In this kitchen, a checkered wall of green and yellow tiles makes a fabulous backdrop for a red and white gingham tablecloth.

► *Mixing and matching checks, plains, and stripes is easy if you keep to the same color theme throughout. In this den, a saffron, green, and white checked sofa forms the basis for the color scheme. The saffron is repeated in the armchair and also in its checked cushion.*

▲ *A checked rug in deep blues and soft pinks looks cozy and welcoming in front of the hearth. You can buy woven or printed checked rugs, or you could paint a checked design onto a plain woven rug yourself. Finish it with a stenciled border around the edges, such as the one on the rug shown here.*

◄ *Blue and white checked cotton teamed with a light wood, such as pine, is a classic country-style combination. Here, four different blue and white checked cottons have been used to frame a set of quaint farmyard animal embroideries, hung above a pine bureau. A matching blue and white checked picture bow sits atop each picture.*

SEEING SPOTS

Perk up your home with cheerful dotted fabrics, wallpaper, and accessories. Use fresh and pretty polka dots on walls and soft furnishings, or make an impact with large, splashy dots on lampshades, crockery, and cushions.

Dots are very simple design motifs, but you'll find endless variations when you look at spotty fabrics, wallpapers, and accessories. There are dots of all sizes, from small, neat polka dots to large, splashy spots. In spotty patterns, the dots can be evenly spaced, scattered at random, or arranged into shapes and motifs. They can be the same size, shape, and color, or an interesting mix. On fabric, the spots can be printed on or woven in.

Dots mix well with many other motifs and patterns, so try combining them with stripes, florals, or checks, and keep a look out for more complex designs that incorporate dots. For example, small to medium-size spots may be used to create a lively but discreet background for a floral or bird motif, making the overall effect more colorful; or a striped or trellis design may be made up of lots of small dots, giving it a softer, less rigid appearance.

◀ *Spotted accessories, like these striking lampshades, add a perky finishing touch to a room.*

▶ *Dots mix well with other patterns if you keep to the same colors. In this cozy corner, fabric and wallpaper with discreet spotted and striped backgrounds are paired with a printed cotton curtain in the same warm, earthy tones.*

USING SPOTS

Spots are so versatile that you can use them anywhere in your home, provided you choose a spotty pattern that suits the setting. Dainty polka dots against a white background are a fresh and pretty choice for bedrooms, bathrooms, and nurseries. They're an easy pattern to live with, so you can use them in abundance on walls and soft furnishings.

Medium to large spots are fun, but need to be used with care, because they can be overpowering. If you're uncertain about using them, either keep to subtle colors or just add a few medium to large spotted accessories to the room, such as lampshades, cushions,

and crockery; if you like the effect, you can always follow through with spotted drapes and upholstery.

You can create a discreetly dotted effect by using a fabric or wallpaper, woven or embossed with dots in a different shade of the same color. For example, hang a polka-dot sheer over a window, so its fine spots are silhouetted against the light.

Using paint, it's easy to create your own spotted patterns. Paint very small freehand dots at random onto a plain jug or vase, or use a spot stencil to create a border on the wall at chair-back height.

◄ There are all sorts of ways to introduce dots into your home. For example, this chair has been deep-buttoned in every color of the rainbow to create a lively pattern of dots. You can create a similar effect by buttoning a cushion. Use buttons all of the same color for a more uniform finish.

► This rustic, earthenware jug painted freehand with a scattering of small blue dots, and crammed full of vivid cornflowers, makes a charming display. Painting a dotted design like this one onto crockery is simple; just use a fine paintbrush to dab spots of special ceramic paint all over the outside of the item.

► *A dotted seat cover brightens up this work corner and links the stool to the blue desk and baseboard. You can make a stool seat cover similar to this one from a circle of fabric with a corded casing around the edge. Just center the fabric over the stool, and then gather it up underneath.*

▼ *The small red dots on this airy sheer curtain look pretty and fresh, silhouetted against the light. They give the fabric a lift, without being overpowering.*

▼ *You can buy dotted crockery, such as this blue and white set, from gift shops and department stores. It makes a lively display on a pine hutch.*

TARTAN FLING

Choose cozy, cheerful tartan for the big warm-up this winter, and surround yourself with bright color combinations and bold checks on fabrics, ceramics, tapestry, and wallpaper – strong designs embodying the comforting traditions of Scotland.

The origins of the beautiful tartans and plaids of Scotland and Ireland are lost in the mists of time, part of a rich Celtic heritage full of romance and myth. These colorful designs were originally the "uniform" by which the many different clans identified each other, not least on the battlefield, for each clan developed its own distinctive design and blend of colors, which were proudly handed down through generations of weavers in the highland crofts. The famous pure wool kilts and plaids were vital for warmth in the cold mountains, but the now-familiar designs have been carried across the world by voyaging and emigrating Celts to be copied and adapted into the culture of many countries far from the Highlands and are now produced in cottons, silks, and linens as well as the original cozy wools. Plaid checks can even be found on metals and ceramics.

TARTAN STYLE
Interior designers have long recognized the importance of these gridlike patterns and blocks of color, and the general structure of the design is often printed onto fabric rather than woven; sometimes painted in a splashy, jazzy style, or blended softly in pastels or neutrals. It often appears as a backdrop to other motifs – garlands of flowers, leaves, and ribbons are thrown into relief by the complex checks.

▶ *For an immediate splash of interest in a tired scheme, you can do no better than a couple of simple cushions in wide-awake colors like these. Rich contrasting primaries are highlighted with strong, black lines, creating rhythmic patterns that draw the eye. You could even base a color scheme on one of these designs, picking out single colors to use in bold swathes around the room for a very contemporary look.*

▼ *A whole room of tartans needs a firm hand and a confident eye, but can have a stunning effect. The odd shape and high window in this room could have a cold and gloomy effect, but a liberal covering of tartan on walls, ceiling, windows, and bed gives an intimate, enclosed feel – just right for a bedroom. The warm red plaid used for the bedspread and curtains contrasts well with the blue-green wallpaper, while a touch of black around the headboard adds definition.*

▲ *Practically everything comes in tartan these days. Snappy plaid mugs are perfect for serving a hot cup of tea; frame your loved ones in Black Watch photo frames to catch the eye; and store your treasures in a smart, plaid jewelry box.*

◀ *Old and scuffed brooms and battered buckets can be given a new lease on life by painting them with a bright tartan pattern.*

DO-IT-YOURSELF TARTAN

These popular and timeless patterns appear regularly on all sorts of articles in modern homes, and many of the ideas are easy to copy with a little time and imagination. Decorate plain china plates with enamel paints to mount in groups on the kitchen wall for instant color; or use durable gloss paints to give your household utensils a cheerful check pattern like the buckets and brushes on the left.

Use tartan gift wrap or tartan cotton fabrics to cover old, worn photograph frames, files, and favorite books for a bright touch of color in an otherwise dark corner, or top a pewter lampbase with a plaid-patterned shade. A big cozy plaid blanket thrown across an old sofa will add instant color to the room and disguise worn patches in one fell swoop, or heap a pile of jewel-bright tartan cushions for the same effect. You could even take tartan into the garden and paint the designs on flowerpots, window boxes, or faded garden furniture.

◄ One of the delights of plaids and tartans is the easy way they mix with other designs and patterns, despite their bold style. This cushion and matching throw both have a vigorous swirling design of colorful flowers and leaves, richly enhanced by the blues, greens, and reds and the gridlike structure of the woolen plaid background.

► The familiar grid design is often used in printed fabrics, using subtle blends of colors to complement floral stablemates. The swagged curtains and tailored armchair in this sitting room blend florals and plaids together for a stylish scheme.

▼ The delicious plaid and roses design of this dinner service is the inspiration for a celebratory table dressed for a special occasion. You may not own a dinner service like this one, but tartan ribbons are an easy and inexpensive way to add instant style to a party table.

BOLD FLORALS

Romantic, daring, and artistic, large floral designs are the inspiration for a variety of furnishing fabrics and wallpapers, painted china, rugs, and artificial flowers. Used with care, there's a place for a bold floral design in every home.

Large floral designs often feature flowers that are naturally large-scale, such as sunflowers, roses, peonies, tulips, and lilies. They can be used in a room scheme to create many different moods. Roses, which are a feature of the cottage or country look, can be soft and romantic, while bright, majestic sunflowers will add a vivid, flamboyant note to a room.

There are many ways to use large florals in the home. Watch for ranges of coordinating fabrics and wallpapers; many include attractive mixes of large florals with other patterns, such as checks and stripes. Be sure to keep an eye out for china decorated with large flowers, floral rugs, out-sized artificial flowers, and floral appliqué, embroidery, and tapestry designs.

Large floral designs with an all-over pattern, where the flower motifs seem to merge together, are easier to use than those whose motifs are distinct and separated by areas of background color. They look effective in traditional homes with high ceilings, where there's enough space to set off windows hung with boldly patterned curtains. In smaller, more modern homes,

however, you will need to be more careful if you're choosing a bold, floral design, because a large pattern may be out of proportion with the scale of the rooms. If this is the case, introduce some accessories that feature large florals instead: a cushion with a huge flower design, or a rug with a bold, floral pattern, for example.

◄ *Hand-painted china is one of the simplest and most effective ways of introducing artistic, large florals into your home. There are many bold and exciting designs to choose from.*

▲ Large florals can work in small rooms if used with care. To avoid the overcrowded look that large, multicolored designs can create, use a one-color fabric print, like the yellow sunflower fabric on this sofa. Add contrast with cushions of the same design but in different colors .

▶ Add instant style to a simply furnished room with a vase of larger-than-life paper flowers. These sunflowers would look good in a blue and yellow room. For a pastel scheme, try giant crêpe-paper roses. It's an idea that works particularly well in an otherwise simply furnished, modern room.

◀ Cover your bed with a profusion of large and medium-sized florals for a soft and inviting look. Continue the theme with a matching wallpaper border and curtains. If you don't feel confident about mixing patterns like this, use one of the ready-made lines specially designed to coordinate in this way.

◀ *This fun cushion is shaped like a flowerpot. It's easy to make one like it: just cut out a few simple flower shapes, leaves, and a pot, then machine-appliqué them onto a fabric backing. Use this as a template to cut out another piece of fabric, and stitch the two together over a filling of wadding.*

▶ *The romance of a rose in full bloom is beautifully captured on this upholstered footstool. The cover is a single motif cut from a very large floral print. It's an excellent way of using a large floral motif in a small room.*

◀ *Warm up a neutral color scheme with a bold, floral rug. The vivid red poppies on a cream background look fresh and bright in this simple living room and do not spoil the room's uncluttered, airy feel.*

~5~

DECORATING TECHNIQUES

COLOR AND TONE

You can use color to create mood, ambience, and atmosphere. It can add warmth to a cold room, cool down a hot one, bring light to a dark corner, and freshen up a gray city apartment. The right color can transform a large, unwelcoming area into a cozy room; it can make a small space feel larger and it can relax or stimulate. Use it to make the most of a favorite feature, such as an attractive fireplace, a beautiful chair, or an elegant window.

When you're choosing colors for a room scheme, do remember that all colors have different tones, depending on how much white, black, or gray has been added to the original hue. The tone affects the color's behavior: for example, the deeper a hot color, the more it advances, and the lighter a cool color, the more it recedes.

Warm colors

These are red, yellow, orange, and red-violet and their various tints, tones, and shades, such as pink, rose, wine, plum, primrose, gold, peach, apricot, rust, terra-cotta, and lilac-pink.

Warm colors are also known as advancing colors; they appear to come toward you, so they make a surface seem closer and an area look smaller. They help to warm up a cold room, set a sunny scene, create a cozy, intimate, or even a stimulating mood.

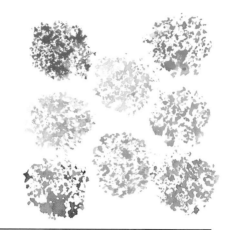

Cool colors

These are blue, green, blue-green, violet, and some cool grays, including all the tonal variations, such as azure, mint, aqua, bottle, olive, sage, blue-lilac, and navy blue.

Cool colors are also known as receding colors. This means they seem to go away from you, making a surface look further away, so the area will appear more spacious and relaxing. They help to cool down a hot room and add style and elegance.

Neutral colors

These are often used as a background or linking color. The true neutral colors are black, white, and gray. Black seems to advance and is dominant in a scheme; white appears to recede and is one of the most successful space-making colors; pale gray will also look spacious, whereas dark gray will be more oppressive.

Other colors that are treated as neutrals – shades like cream, beige, golden-brown, and off-white – are known as naturals because they are found in products like wood, stone, cotton, flax, slate, cane, and rush.

Neutrals and naturals can be warm or cool, depending on how close they are to the warm creams, yellows, and orange, or to gray-blues and greens. They are nonconfrontational, creating a relaxing atmosphere.

Using tones

When you've chosen a basic color scheme, the next step is to think about tones. Tones are vital: light, medium, and dark tones affect the shape and balance of a room in different ways, even more than colors themselves. Most rooms have good points that can be highlighted and bad points that can be disguised. Study these diagrams to see how you can do this. If you like, trace the diagrams and color them in to see how the different tones affect your own color scheme.

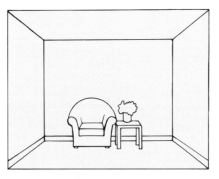

To make a room seem larger, use light colors – the lighter the color, the more spacious the room feels.

To make a room feel smaller or cozier, use warm colors to bring the walls and ceiling inward.

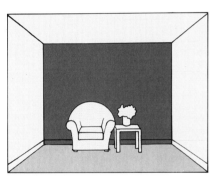

To make a wall seem closer, decorate it in a dark, warm color so that it comes toward you.

To make a wall or ceiling look further away, decorate it in a cool, pale, receding color.

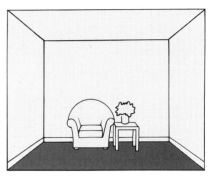

To make the floor seem smaller, choose a dark floor covering. This also draws the eye downward.

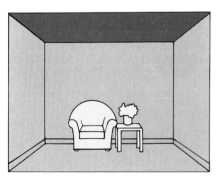

To lower a ceiling, paint it a little darker than the walls. Don't paint it too dark, or it will seem oppressive.

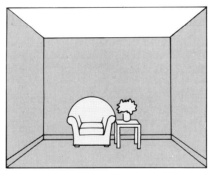

To make a ceiling seem higher, paint it lighter than the walls – white is a popular choice.

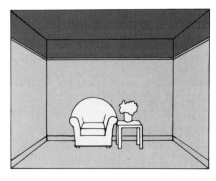

To lower the ceiling in a large room, paint the top of the walls in the same dark color as the ceiling.

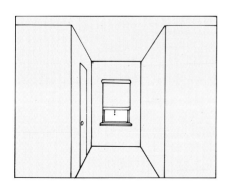

To widen a corridor, use a very light, cool color on the walls, ceiling, and floor. The reflected light will make the area look less confined.

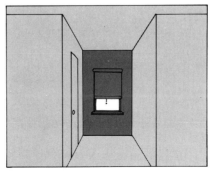

To shorten a corridor or a long, narrow room, paint the end wall in a dark or warm color. This makes it look closer.

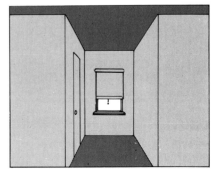

To make a corridor or room look lower and wider, decorate the ceiling and floor in a darker or warmer shade than the walls.

PREPARING WOOD FOR PAINTING

Wooden surfaces, such as doors, banisters, and windows, get a lot of hard wear. If you are going to paint them, you need to prepare them. This will ensure that the paint looks good and lasts as long as possible. Here is a guide to preparing both used and new wood for painting.

ASSESSING THE SURFACE

First decide how much preparation you need to do. In most cases, you'll be working on old paint. If it's in reasonable condition, all you'll need to do is sand it and wash it.

Small flaws, like cracks and holes and flaking paint, need filling and sanding. You'll need to strip the paint only if it is in very bad condition, or if you want to give it a clear finish, with stain or varnish. If the wood is new you'll need to sand it smooth, seal any knots, and then prime it.

EQUIPMENT

Sandpaper. Keep a selection of fine, medium, and coarse grades to abrade painted surfaces and to remove old paint. Use finer sandpaper when you get to the wood.

Fillers. For filling cracks and holes in wood, choose a *cellulose filler*, which comes in powder or putty form. *Plastic wood* comes in a range of finishes to match common wood types such as pine, mahogany, and teak. Use this for a clear finish.

Filling knife. Like a putty knife, this tool has a flexible blade and is used to force filler into cracks and holes.

Sanding block. Wrap sandpaper around a cork or wood block for a good grip and for even sanding.

Scraper. Use a scraper with a small blade, about 1in (2.5cm) wide, for removing old paint from windows, doors, etc.

Shavehooks. These are used to strip off paint. Use a shavehook with a *triangular blade* for flat surfaces. Use a *combination blade* to scrape paint from small and molded or curved areas.

Other equipment. You'll also need a plastic bucket and a sponge plus degreaser, soda crystals dissolved in hot water, or detergent for washing paintwork. An old toothbrush is useful for reaching hard-to-access areas. Wear rubber gloves to protect your hands when washing the paintwork.

shavehook-triangular blade

shavehook-combination blade

scraper

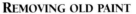

PREPARING EXISTING PAINT

If the paint is in good condition, rub it down with sandpaper to roughen the surface and help the new paint to adhere. Then wash it down to remove dust and grease.

1 WASHING THE SURFACE
Sponge on a degreaser or solution of hot water and washing soda or detergent to remove dirt and grease. Use an old toothbrush in crevices and corners. Rinse the surface and let it dry.

REMOVING OLD PAINT

Most paintwork has some holes, chips, cracks, and flaking areas that must be repaired. New paint will not stick to old paint that's flaking away. It will fill hairline cracks and pinholes but anything larger, if left unfilled, will show through the new coat. After correcting these flaws, sand and wash the surface (see PREPARING EXISTING PAINT).

BARE PATCHES
Seal any bare patches of wood with acrylic primer or latex paint. Use several coats to build up the level to match the existing paint.

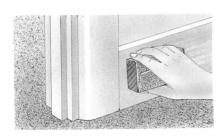

2 SANDING THE SURFACE
Using a sanding block and fine-grade sandpaper, rub along the surface, following the direction of the wood grain underneath the paint. On curves, hold the paper in your hand. Sand evenly until the paint is no longer glossy. Then wipe away the dust.

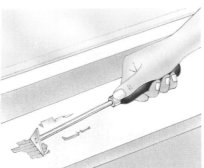

REMOVING FLAKING PAINT
Use coarse sandpaper and a shavehook: pull the tool firmly over the surface to take off the paint without damaging the wood. Then sand the surface and wipe away the dust.

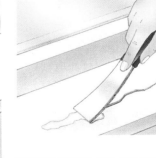

FILLING HOLES AND CRACKS
Fill any holes and cracks with wood filler. Make a stiff mixture, following the manufacturer's instructions, then press it into the flaws, using a flexible filling knife. Scrape off any excess filler immediately, or let it dry and then sand it flat.

Stripping paint

If the paintwork is in poor condition generally, or if you want to replace it with a clear finish, you'll need to strip it all off. The best methods involve softening the paint with heat or chemicals and then stripping it away. For most woodwork, a power-tool sanding attachment is unsuitable because it is difficult to use on ledges, corners, and curves. It will also create a lot of unwelcome dust.

Heat. The quickest way to soften paint is to burn it off with a blowtorch, but this method has some disadvantages. You may get unsightly scorch marks on the wood, and the heat may crack window panes. You could try using an electric hot-air stripper. This is a much gentler method, but it can still crack glass if not used carefully.
Liquid chemical stripper. This is an effective way to remove one or two layers of paint, but for thicker paint-work, you'll need several applications to remove all the paint.
Paste chemical stripper. This is used in the same way as liquid chemical stripper, but it is much thicker. It can remove several layers of paint at once. It adheres well, so it is a good choice for stripping vertical surfaces such as doors and wall panels. It's more expensive than liquid paint stripper.

USING A BLOWTORCH

Work from the bottom upward and keep the flame constantly moving to avoid scorching the wood. As soon as the paint bubbles up, scrape it off, moving the flame onward. At all times, be very careful where you are pointing the naked flame. Sand the surface with medium-grade sandpaper to remove odd spots of paint and any light scorch marks, and to smooth it out.

USING A HOT-AIR STRIPPER

Holding the hot-air gun about 2in (5cm) away from the surface, move it slowly backward and forward until the paint bubbles up and can be scraped off. When working next to glass, keep the tool moving and use the special flat nozzles provided to aim the hot air away from the glass. Alternatively, use a chemical stripper next to glass. Finally, sand the wood smooth.

USING CHEMICAL STRIPPER

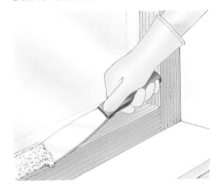

Follow the manufacturer's instructions, leaving the stripper on long enough to soften the paint. With liquid stripper this usually takes 10-15 minutes (or even less in very warm weather); paste can take some hours. Scrape the surface clean and rinse it with water or mineral spirits to neutralize the stripper. Let it dry, then sand it smooth.

A clear finish

A clear finish does not conceal imperfections, so your preparation work must be careful and thorough. When you are stripping paint for a clear finish, use a chemical stripper or a hot-air gun, rather than a blowtorch, to avoid any scorch marks. If you want to strip a door, you could remove it and send it off to be dipped. However, dipping can weaken the joints, so make sure your door is in good condition before sending it off.

On old timber, you may encounter a bottom layer of paint that refuses to budge. Try rubbing this down with steel wool dipped in chemical stripper.

If the wood needs filling, use matching plastic wood, not white cellulose filler. Finally, sand the wood down with medium sandpaper, then finish with fine sandpaper.

PREPARING UNPAINTED WOOD

New wood and wood that has been stripped must be sanded smooth and sealed before it is painted.

1 SEALING KNOTS
Scrape off any hardened resin. If the wood is to be painted, seal every knot with two coats of shellac. If the wood is to have a clear finish, seal the knots with a slightly thinned coat of the varnish.

2 PREPARING TO PAINT
When it's dry, sand the wood smooth with fine sandpaper, slightly rounding off any sharp edges to help the paint adhere. If you are going to paint the wood, seal it with a suitable acrylic primer.

QUICK WORK

With existing paint that's in good condition, you can simply wash and coat in one step with liquid sander, a mildly abrasive cleaner that slightly roughens the surface, leaving it ready for recoating.

WAXING AND OILING WOOD

For centuries, wax and oil have been used to finish wood. They don't give as much protection as modern varnishes and take time to apply and maintain, but give wood a beautiful, traditional luster.

Follow the steps to use oil or wax to give a traditional look to wooden surfaces, or to revive an old oiled or waxed finish.

OIL FINISHES

Oil gives wood a soft, satin sheen that is tough and durable. Oiled surfaces resist water and alcohol and, to some extent, heat, so this finish is suitable for tables and other household surfaces.

The finish is achieved by rubbing in layers of oil, leaving the wood to dry between each layer. You can use oil only on new or totally stripped wood or previously oiled wood.

Oils. Traditionally, *linseed oil* was used. It's very slow-drying, so use one of the faster-drying modern oils, such as *teak oil* or *Danish oil*. These take about four hours to dry, so you can build up the required coatings more quickly. Teak oil gives a higher sheen than Danish oil.

WAX FINISHES

Wax gives wood a beautiful, easy-to-maintain finish. Waxed surfaces can be marked by heat and water, and they get dirty easily because the wax makes them slightly sticky, so use wax on items that won't get much wear and tear, such as decorative storage boxes. Wax can be applied to new or newly stripped wood or to oiled surfaces.

Beeswax. The most widely used wax finish, this varies in color from pale yellow to orange-brown. You can also buy bleached (white) beeswax and colored waxes for an antique effect.

Carnauba wax. Harder than beeswax, this provides a high, long-lasting gloss finish. It is often added to beeswax to reduce its slight tackiness and improve its durability.

Paraffin wax. A soft wax, widely used in cheaper polishes, it is sometimes added to high-quality wax polishes to make them softer and easier to apply.

Preparing new wood

New wood needs very little preparation before it's oiled or waxed: just sand it lightly with flour-grade (fine) abrasive paper, then wipe it over with a cloth moistened with mineral spirits to remove the dust. This will also help to remove any excess natural oils from oily woods like teak.

Preparing old wood

Old wood is often marked or damaged: common marks include fine scratches and a build-up of dirt, ring marks, and cigarette burns. If the damage is only surface-deep, you can clean it up with mineral spirits and polish reviver, then apply fresh wax polish (see OLD WAXED WOOD, below). However, if the wood beneath the surface is damaged, you'll need to repair the blemishes.

OLD WAXED WOOD

Follow these step-by-step instructions to clean and revive old waxed wood, ready for a new coat of wax.

> ### MATERIALS
> **Clean rags and mineral spirits**
> **Polish reviver**
> **Fine steel wool (optional)**
> **Wax**
> **Metal polish or ring remover**

1 CLEANING THE SURFACE
Moisten a cloth with mineral spirits and rub it over the surface. If the finish is hard to remove, use the steel wool to rub gently in the direction of the grain.

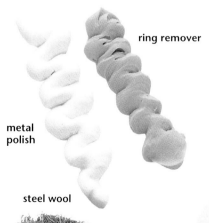

ring remover

metal polish

steel wool

2 REMOVING STAINS
Remove drink rings and other watermarks by rubbing the surface with metal polish or commercially available ring remover. If the stain has penetrated to the wood, or if the surface is deeply scratched or burnt, you will have to strip down to the bare wood (see page 141).

3 APPLYING THE REVIVER
Following the manufacturer's instructions, apply the polish reviver to the wooden surface, then apply a fresh coat of wax.

mineral spirits

polish reviver

cloth

WAXED AND OILED WOOD

Using very fine, 000-gauge, steel wool dipped in mineral spirits, rub the wood to remove the old finish.

FRENCH POLISH

Using very fine, 000-gauge, steel wool, rub mineral spirits over the wood to remove the old finish.

POLYURETHANE FINISHES

Use a solvent-based varnish remover or paint stripper to remove the finish, since water-based types will raise the grain of the wood, creating more work. Apply the remover sparingly, following the manufacturer's instructions. Remove the softened residue with a paint scraper or steel wool. Neutralize the stripper thoroughly by scrubbing the surface with mineral spirits.

CELLULOSE FINISHES

Remove these in the same way as polyurethane finishes.

PAINT FINISHES

Strip the paint using a blowtorch, hot-air stripper, or a chemical stripper (see page 141).

DEALING WITH STAINS AND BLEMISHES

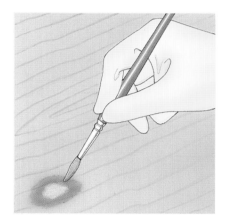

DARK STAINS

Bleach out the stain using commercially available wood bleach, hydrogen peroxide, or a solution of 1 tablespoon (15ml) of oxalic acid in 1 pint (½ liter) of water.

These treatments will also lighten the surrounding wood, so either bleach the whole surface or restore the original color with wood stains.

INK STAINS

Sand the stain, then bleach the area with a two-part bleach or a strong solution of oxalic acid: dissolve 1 tablespoon of oxalic acid crystals in 2 tablespoons (30ml) of boiling water. Wearing rubber gloves, apply the bleach with a pad of cotton wool. Leave it for a few minutes, then repeat, if necessary.

BURNS

Scrape away the charred wood using a sharp knife. Then sand the area smooth and apply several coats of finish to fill in the slight hollow. Alternatively, use a commercially available scratch remover, following the manufacturer's instructions. With deep depressions, you may need to use colored beeswax as a filler first.

DENTS

Use boiling water to swell the wood fibers. In order to do this, simply boil a kettle, then sprinkle a few drops of water from the kettle over the dent, being careful not to scald yourself. Allow the wood to dry out completely before applying the finish.

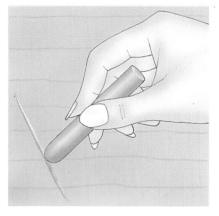

SCRATCHES

Fill scratches with commercially available wax furniture crayon in a color to match the wood. Alternatively, melt colored beeswax (available in small sticks) into the scratches. Let the filler harden, then shave off the excess wax with a razor blade.

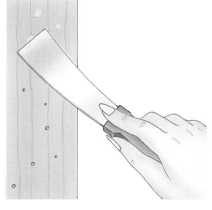

WOODWORM

Treat the holes with a commercially available woodworm treatment, following manufacturer's instructions. Then fill the holes with plastic wood, using a flexible knife on flat surfaces and a cloth on turned areas. Let the filler harden, and sand it smooth.

LIMING WOOD

The simple, decorative technique known as liming gives a silvery, bleached appearance to wood and highlights the pattern of the grain. It is best suited to woods with an open grain, such as oak and ash. Pine can also be limed, but it requires more preparation to open up the grain.

New and old wood can be treated in this way, but remember that liming has to be applied to bare wood, so any finishes – paint, varnish, or polish – must be removed before you start.

LIMING TECHNIQUES

Traditionally, limewash was used for liming, but since this is caustic and therefore quite dangerous, two modern techniques, using either liming wax or white eggshell paint, are now preferred. These alternatives are safe, readily available and very easy to use; they are both equally effective, but you'll find that liming wax produces a slightly more subtle effect.

To create a colored, limed effect, use either colored eggshell paint, or white eggshell paint tinted with universal stainers or any artists' oil paints. Mix them together in a jam jar and test the paint on a scrap of wood before starting your project. For best results, use soft, pale shades – pale blue-grays and green-grays are popular and work well with many color schemes.

PREPARING THE WOOD

As with many decorating techniques, the success of liming depends on the preparation carried out beforehand. All surface finishes must be removed before liming so that the bare wood is exposed. For information on how to remove existing paint finishes, refer to pages 140–41.

Preparing wood for liming can be very messy, so either work outside or use a lot of newspapers to cover the floor. Wear old clothes and rubber gloves, and use some form of nose and mouth protection.

Raising the grain

When the surface is clean and, as near as possible, returned to its natural wood color, you will need to open up the grain of the wood with a decorator's stiff-wire brush.

> **MATERIALS**
> Wooden object for liming
> Decorator's stiff-wire brush
> Lint-free, cotton cloths
> Medium-grade sandpaper

1 WETTING THE WOOD
Working on a small area at a time, wipe the surface of the wood with cold water and let it soak in for a few minutes. This softens the fibers of the wood grain.

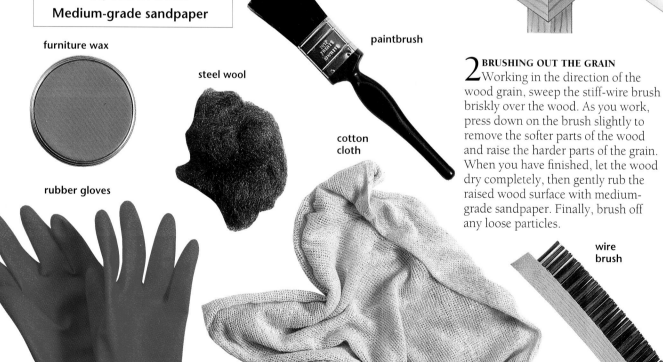

furniture wax

rubber gloves

steel wool

paintbrush

cotton cloth

white paint

wire brush

2 BRUSHING OUT THE GRAIN
Working in the direction of the wood grain, sweep the stiff-wire brush briskly over the wood. As you work, press down on the brush slightly to remove the softer parts of the wood and raise the harder parts of the grain. When you have finished, let the wood dry completely, then gently rub the raised wood surface with medium-grade sandpaper. Finally, brush off any loose particles.

Liming with paint

After you have opened the wood grain, use household eggshell paint to produce a limed effect. If you would like the finished project to have a slight sheen, buff on some furniture wax, or, for more durable protection, apply one or two coats of matte or gloss varnish.

MATERIALS

White or tinted eggshell paint

Mineral spirits

Lint-free, soft cotton cloths

Fine steel wool (000 grade)

Furniture wax or household varnish (optional)

Rubber gloves

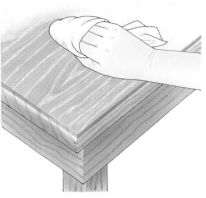

1 APPLYING THE PAINT
Wearing rubber gloves, dip a cloth into the paint and rub the paint well into the grain of the wood. Cover the entire surface in this way, making sure you work the paint into all the corners.

2 REMOVING THE PAINT
Lightly dampen a clean cloth with mineral spirits. Stretch the cloth across your fingers and rub off the excess paint, leaving color in the grain only. Let dry.

3 FINISHING
Either leave the surface as it is or apply a wax or varnish finish.

Liming with wax

Liming wax is applied to wood that you have prepared first by removing any finishes and raising the grain. To enhance the natural soft sheen that you get with liming wax, buff on some furniture wax. You can buy liming wax from paint stores and arts and crafts shops.

MATERIALS

Liming wax

Furniture wax

Fine steel wool (000 grade)

Lint-free, soft cotton cloths

Clean, dry brush

Rubber gloves

1 APPLYING THE WAX
Wearing rubber gloves, pull off a piece of steel wool and dip it into the liming wax. Using a circular motion, rub the wax into the wood, working both with and against the grain. Each time the steel wool pad you are using becomes completely soaked with wax, throw it away and use a fresh piece. Work until all the indentations in the wood grain are filled and you have covered the surface of the object.

2 TAKING EFFECT
Leave the wax on for about 30 minutes for a fairly subtle effect, or up to 1 hour for a stronger, grainier finish.

3 REMOVING THE WAX
Take a fresh piece of fine steel wool, dip it into the furniture wax, and rub this over the surface of the wood in the direction of the grain. Work until you have removed all the liming wax from the surface of the wood, leaving the grain clearly marked in white.

4 FINISHING
Dust off any loose particles with the brush. Then, using a soft cloth, apply a layer of wax furniture polish. Buff the wax with another clean cloth to produce a soft sheen.

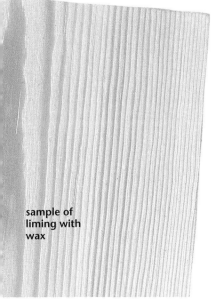

sample of liming with wax

sample of liming with tinted paint

PAINTS AND VARNISHES

There are two questions to ask when choosing a paint or varnish: will it produce the effect you want, and is it right for the surface? This guide to paints and varnishes for *indoor* use outlines the properties of the various types commonly available.

TYPES OF PAINT

Oil-based paints. These are durable, glossy paints, now made with a synthetic resin called alkyd rather than with traditional oils such as linseed. They can be used full-strength or diluted with solvent and colored for special effects. A wide range of colors are available. Gloss and eggshell may need an undercoat. They are slow drying and give off unpleasant fumes.

Water-based paints. Only water-based paints made with synthetic resins are covered in the following table. These are waterproof and quite durable, quick drying, easy to apply, and come in a wide range of colors.

Solvent-based paints. Coatings and colorings that are solvent-based tend to be fragile.

Varnish. A transparent, protective coating that comes in gloss, semigloss, and matte finishes. Clear varnish can have colors added; ready-mixed colored varnishes are also available.

Other types of paint. Several other types of paint and coloring agents can be used on a variety of surfaces. Fabric, carpet, and leather dyes aren't listed below, but they are worth trying out as coloring agents, particularly on bare wood surfaces.

TYPES OF FINISH

Many coatings are sold in three types of finish – gloss, semigloss, and matte.
Gloss. This is a tough, water-resistant finish with a high sheen, ideal for areas subject to heavy wear.
Semigloss. Also called silk, satin, or eggshell, this is less shiny and less durable than gloss. The paints can often resist dampness and be wiped clean.
Matte. This provides a low-glare finish that is the least durable.

PRIMER AND UNDERCOAT

Surfaces sometimes require a preparatory coating of primer and undercoat before their decorative coating.
Primers. These seal porous surfaces such as raw plaster or wood and provide adhesion on surfaces like bare metal. For metals, such as steel and aluminum, there are special primers that prevent rust.
Emulsion primer. This is suitable for most household surfaces except metal. It is almost odorless and quick drying.

NONDRIP PAINT

Nondrip paint is easy to use and ideal for ceilings, but don't stir it even if there are lumps, because it will turn to liquid and lose its nondrip quality.

Undercoat. This is painted over primer. It is also used where the present color or paint type on a surface is very different from the new paint. It contains more pigment than topcoat paint and dries to a semimatte finish that gives depth of color to the final coating. Most paint suppliers will suggest an appropriate undercoat color.

PRACTICAL POINTS

Remember to use the correct solvent when thinning paint or cleaning brushes (water for water-based paints, mineral spirits for oil and solvent-based paints).

To store paint or varnish, replace the lid and, provided it closes well, turn the can upside down to form a seal.

Don't dispose of unwanted paint and solvent down sinks or drains. Find out if your town has disposal facilities, or put them out with your household rubbish in clearly marked containers.

TYPE	USES	MIX WITH	QUALITIES
OIL-BASED PAINTS			
Gloss	Wood and furniture—dilute to make a hard-wearing wash	Universal stainers, artist's oil paints, transparent oil glaze	Tough, glossy finish but shows up flaws
Eggshell	Good nonabsorbent base for a glaze—use for dragging, ragging, sponging, and stenciling on wood	As above	Durable finish between gloss and matte—good for rough surfaces
Undercoat	Gives depth of color to the topcoat	Universal stainers, artist's oil paints	Not intended as a decorative coating but can be tinted with artist's colors to give a matte finish
Lacquer	Wood and furniture	Not applicable	Highly glossy, waterproof finish—flows onto surface easily; dries quickly so more than one coat can be applied in a day
Artist's oil paints	Coloring oil-based paint, glaze, and varnish	As above plus beeswax polish and turpentine for an antique finish	Intense colors, slow drying—so especially good for beginners
Transparent oil glaze	Stippling, dragging, rag-rolling, wood-graining, and antiquing	Tint with artist's oils or universal stainers; for a subtle look, thin with mineral spirits	Sometimes called scumble glaze, dries slowly, allowing time to work on the finish; yellows with age and when exposed to sunlight

TYPE	USES	MIX WITH	QUALITIES
WATER-BASED			
Emulsion	Generally used for walls and ceilings but not wood, because it raises the grain	Artist's acrylic paints, universal stainers, powder paint	Comes in all finishes, often described as matte, silk, and satin sheen—dark colors lack depth
Artist's acrylic paints	Painting small items, stenciling on wood, or fabric and coloring washes	Emulsion	Bright colors, easy to use, and dries fast to a rich, glossy finish—doesn't need primer or undercoat; clean brush immediately after use
Powder paint	Use to make own paint for color-washing or as tinting agent	Emulsion, transparent oil glaze, oil-based, and polyurethane varnish	Needs protective finish—can be very toxic
SOLVENT-BASED			
Glass paint	For painting glass, china, and pottery	Special glass paint thinner, if required	On glass gives a stained-glass effect; on china and pottery produces a translucent finish—thick sticky paints are tricky to use and must be applied in a dust-free atmosphere; scratches easily; not suitable for heavy wear
Ceramic paint	Painting clay, pottery, glass, metal, wood	Turpentine or water, depending on the base	Gives a glossy, opaque, delicate finish. Use with ceramic varnish to protect the design
Universal stainers	Dyes that can be added to nearly all finishes, from emulsion to wood stain	See uses	Intense colors that come in liquid form and mix well with other solutions
VARNISH			
Polyurethane	An all-purpose varnish for walls, woodwork, floors, and furniture	Oil-based paints, artist's oils, powder paints, and oil glaze	Easy to use—gives a hard, long-lasting coating to almost anything; dries in 4-6 hours
Acrylic	Good for all types of decorative varnish	Water-based paints, universal stainers, and powder colors	Tough, durable, clear; quick-drying; easy to use. Two types: water-based and petroleum distillate-based (latter highly toxic, to be avoided)
OTHER PAINTS			
Aerosol paints	Polyurethane or enamel spray paints that can be used on most surfaces—good for stenciling and other decorative effects	Not applicable	Hard, very smooth finish—fast to apply; quick-drying; unpleasant, toxic fumes
Wood stain	Use oil-based stains for softwoods and water-based wood stains on light or fine-grained woods	Mineral spirits or water, depending on the base	Oil-based stains more transparent than water stains; color penetrates evenly; takes any clear finish when dry; dries slowly. Water-based stain lifts the grain; must be rubbed down before sealing and waxing
Liming wax	Gives wood a bleached look while emphasizing the grain—especially good on pine and oak	Not applicable	Produces a softer sheen than other methods of liming
Stencil paint	Stenciling	Not applicable	Dries almost instantly, minimizing risk of smudges

STENCILING

This technique is a simple and effective way to paint a motif or even a continuous border onto a wall, an object, or piece of furniture. A cutout shape, is placed on a surface and then paint is brushed, sponged, or sprayed over the cutout area. When the stencil is removed, the motif remains.

WHERE TO USE STENCILS

Stencils can be used to decorate many surfaces, such as walls, ceilings, floors, furniture, household objects, and fabric. Surfaces should be clean, sound, and, for an even stencil, preferably smooth.

TYPES OF STENCILS

Many companies produce stencils made in metal, oiled card, or clear acetate film. Some ready-made stencils are precut. Others, which are sold uncut, are cheaper but less convenient. For designs with more than one color, there is usually a separate stencil for each color.

Make your own stencil using either oiled manila card or acetate. Manila card is easier to cut, but acetate is transparent, so it is easier to position accurately, and it will bend around a curved surface.

Commercial stencils and kits are sold in home furnishing departments, and art stores. Acetate and oiled manila card are sold in arts and crafts stores.

SUITABLE PAINTS

The paint must be suitable for the object being stenciled. To reduce the risk of the stencil smudging, use a quick-drying paint where possible. You need only a small amount of paint for stenciling – "test" pots are ideal.

For walls painted with emulsion, use emulsion or artist's acrylics (which are water-based). Artist's acrylics are a good choice; they are readily available in a wide range of colors and are sold in small tubes. On fabric, use special fabric paints from craft or hobby shops.

To stencil on a surface painted with an oil-based paint, use an oil-based paint, such as eggshell. As a tip, if you are painting woodwork to be stenciled, use a medium-sheen oil-based paint. A full-gloss paint is very difficult to stencil, since it provides poor adhesion for the new stencil paint.

VARNISH

Stencils on surfaces that will be subject to heavy wear need to be protected with varnish. Use a clear matte or gloss polyurethane varnish, and apply it two to three days after stenciling.

OTHER MATERIALS

Brushes. Stencil brushes are round, with short stiff bristles, and they give a softly stippled finish. Alternatively, use a blunt-ended hogshair artist's brush, or a stiff decorating brush. You will need one brush for each color, and the size of the brushes should be in proportion to the size of the stencil motif: for instance, do not attempt to stencil a small design with a large brush or vice versa.

Chalk. This is useful for marking the position of a stencil on a wall.

Craft knife. Used to cut out the stencil.

Cutting board. These are sold in office supply shops and are the ideal surface to cut out a stencil. Alternatively, use a piece of hardboard.

Insulating tape. This is useful for repairing a stencil.

Saucers. Use old plates or saucers for holding the paint.

Sponges. Both synthetic and natural sponges can be used to apply the paint, and they give a pleasing, dappled look.

Scrap card and paper. This is for practicing and for removing excess paint from the brush or sponge.

Tape measure or ruler. This is to position the stencil accurately.

stenciling brushes

oiled manila card stencil

craft knife

acetate stencil

metal stencil

stenciling brush

sponge

HOW TO STENCIL WITH A BRUSH

The real charm of stenciling is its simple, hand-done look, so don't worry if you make the odd mistake; it will add character. Practice on paper first – you can use it later as wrapping paper or to make a greeting card.

MATERIALS	
Stencil	Masking tape
Item to stencil	Saucer
Suitable paint	Scrap paper and rags or paper towel
Chalk or pencil	
Small round stencil brush	Mineral spirits (if using oil-based paint)

CUTTING OUT A STENCIL

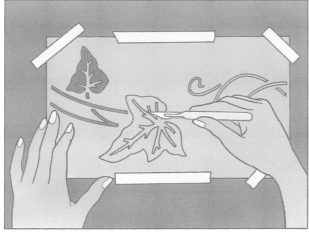

Uncut stencils have the motif or design marked on them for you to cut out. Fix the stencil securely to a cutting board with masking tape, then use a craft knife to cut out the areas to be painted. Cut out any small detailed sections first.

Take your time. To avoid jagged edges, always draw the knife toward you and keep going for the entire length of a cutting line. When cutting curves, turn the board rather than the knife for a smoother cut.

If the stencil is made of card, finish off by smoothing down any rough edges with very fine sandpaper.

USING A STENCIL

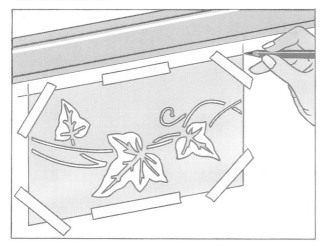

1 Mark positions for the stencil with chalk or pencil. Tape the stencil firmly in place. When you use tape on a wall or paper, first remove some of the tape's stickiness by pressing it onto your forearm a few times.

2 Pour a little paint into a saucer. It should have a creamy consistency. If it is too thin it will seep under the edge of the stencil. If necessary, dilute it with a little water (water-based paints) or mineral spirits (oil-based paints).

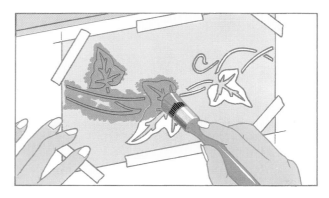

3 Dip the end of the brush into the paint and remove any excess paint on scrap paper. The brush should be almost dry. Hold the brush at a right angle to the surface and use a dabbing motion to apply the paint. Work from the outside of the cutout areas to the center. To stop the paint seeping under the edges, gently press the stencil flat against the surface with your free hand as you work.

4 Let the paint dry. Remove the tape and lift off the stencil. Do not slide it off or you may smudge the paint.

5 Complete the design in the first color. At regular intervals, wipe the stencil and the brush clean with a tissue or rag moistened with water (or mineral spirits for oil-based paint) to prevent a build-up of paint.

6 Let the first color dry completely then start again with the next color. Carefully position the stencil, so that it is registered with the first color. Tape it in place and, using a clean brush, apply the paint as for the first stencil. Repeat this if using more than two colors.

PAINTING FLOORS

One simple and inexpensive way to decorate floors is to paint them. You can paint floorboards or plywood sheeting any color you like, and then varnish over the top to create a surprisingly durable, wipe-clean finish. The steps for preparing the floor, painting it, and applying the varnish are for wooden floors only. If you're painting a concrete floor, you'll find full instructions on page 151.

CHOOSING PAINT

Painting a floor is a big job so, to save time, use paints that are easy to apply, quick-drying, and, ideally, that don't need primer and/or undercoat. It's best not to use solvent-based gloss paint, because it gives off unpleasant fumes and it needs extra sanding before you apply the varnish over the top.

CHOOSING VARNISH

Choose a matte or satin-finish varnish, since high-gloss varnishes can be slippery underfoot. Make sure the varnish is hard-wearing – polyurethane is ideal – and check that it's compatible with the paint you're using.

The more layers of varnish you apply, the more hard-wearing the finish will be. Ideally, you'll need a minimum of three coats. As a rough guide, 35fl oz (1 liter) of varnish will cover 160sq ft (15sq m) per coat.

MATERIALS

Paint for the top coat

Varnish

Primer (optional)

Undercoat (optional)

Sandpaper

Wood filler

3in (75mm) paintbrush

3in (75mm) varnish brush

Mineral spirits

Lint-free cloths

Hammer

Claw hammer or pincers

Nail punch

Vacuum cleaner

Preparing the floor

For good results, it's vital to prepare the floor thoroughly. Remove all the furniture and floor coverings first.

GAPS BETWEEN FLOORBOARDS
If there are gaps between the floorboards, don't try to fill them; it will take too long and the filling is likely to fall out. Instead, lift the boards and re-lay them with the gaps closed up, adding new boards to fill in the extra space you've created. Alternatively, cover the floorboards with sheets of plywood: pin them at 6in (15cm) intervals right across each sheet.

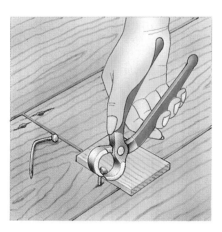

REMOVING OLD FLOOR FIXINGS
Using a claw hammer or pincers, remove any pins, tacks, nails, or staples used to secure previous floor coverings. Protect the floor while you're doing this with a scrap of wood or thick cardboard. Use a hot-air gun to soften old adhesive, then scrape it off. Unfortunately, it's virtually impossible to remove the black bitumen-based adhesive often used in Victorian times, and you can't paint over it because the bitumen will show through the paint.

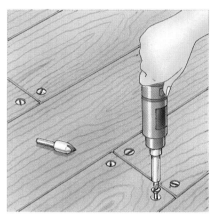

LOOSE FLOORBOARDS
Nail down any loose boards. If any boards are warped, screw them down flat onto the joist beneath. You'll need screws at least double the thickness of the floorboard – 1½in (38mm) screws are adequate for most floorboards. Use a twist drill bit to drill the screw holes, then use a countersink bit to make a recess for the screw heads.

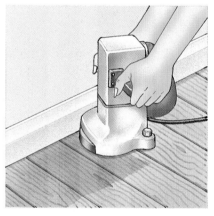

REMOVING FINISHES
If your floor has a painted or stained finish, strip the floor using a blow-torch or a hot-air stripper. Alternatively, sand it with a drum sander and disc or belt sander.

SMALL BLEMISHES
Use a hammer and nail punch to drive any nails below the surface. Fill over any remaining nail holes and screw heads, knot holes, and other small blemishes with wood filler. Leave the filler slightly above the surface, then sand it down flush when it has set.

Applying the paint

1 CLEANING THE SURFACE
Vacuum the prepared floor surface thoroughly, then wipe it down with a lint-free cloth moistened with mineral spirits to lift any remaining dust.

2 PREPARATION (OPTIONAL)
If the paint you are using requires primer and/or undercoat, apply this first. When the primer is thoroughly dry, gently rub it smooth with fine-grade sandpaper. Then apply the undercoat. Start at the wall furthest from the room door and cover the area around the door last.

3 PAINTING THE FLOOR
Apply the paint generously to each board in turn, in the direction of the grain. Work the paint into the gaps between the boards, but don't flood them. Let the paint dry and apply a second coat, if necessary.

Applying the varnish

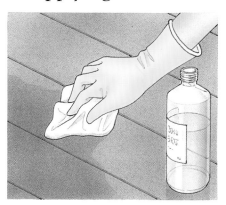

1 PREPARING THE FLOOR
Sand the floor surface lightly with fine abrasive paper to remove specks of dust trapped in the paint and to flatten wood fibers raised by water-based paint. Wipe the surface with a lint-free cloth soaked in mineral spirits to remove the sanding dust.

2 VARNISHING THE FLOOR
Apply a generous coat of varnish, working in the direction of the grain. Let it dry for 2 hours.

3 APPLYING ADDITIONAL COATS
Sand the surface lightly to provide adhesion, then apply another coat of varnish and let it dry thoroughly. Apply at least three coats of varnish in this way, sanding lightly between coats.

Painting concrete floors

If you want to paint a concrete floor, use one of the special floor paints designed for concrete. You can apply concrete paints directly onto the surface, so you won't need primer or undercoat. These paints are hard-wearing, so there's no need for a protective coat of varnish on top.

If the concrete floor is newly laid, let it dry out for three months before painting it.

PAINTING CONCRETE
Repair any cracks and holes in the concrete before you paint it. If the floor is damp, treat this first. Then scrub the floor with a solution of washing soda or degreaser, and rinse it, taking care not to overwet the concrete. Apply the paint around the edges using a large brush, following the manufacturer's instructions. Paint the center using a paint roller with an extension handle.

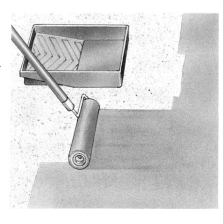

SIMPLE PAINT EFFECTS

If you've got plain painted walls, woodwork, or accessories, you can give them a new look with simple paint effects. There's a wide range of effects to choose from. If you're a beginner, you'll find broken-color techniques easiest to do.

Broken-color techniques start with a plain, base color. You then create a pattern over it using a second and sometimes a third color.

Traditionally, a tinted glaze was used to create the pattern over the base color. However, with some broken-color effects, such as sponging, you can get good results with emulsion. You'll find details of suitable paints in the instructions for each technique.

Before you start, try out different color combinations using test pots or artist's paints. For more subtle effects, choose either two similar colors, or two shades of the same color, applying the lighter one first. For a more dramatic effect, use two shades of a strong color, such as deep terra-cotta. Avoid using two very different colors, like yellow and dark green; the effect can be jarring.

When you are painting walls, start on a window wall, where a beginner's mistakes will be much less noticeable. Always paint at least a whole wall in one session, stopping if necessary at a corner. If you stop in the middle of a wall, the dried edge may show when you've finished.

BASE COAT

Use oil-based paint, such as eggshell or gloss, or use vinyl silk, which is water-based, so it's easy to work with.

TOP COAT

Glaze. This gives the most professional finish. It is transparent, so the base color shows through it, giving the finished effect greater depth. It's oil-based, so it takes some time to dry, giving you longer to work.

You can buy special paint-effect glazes in a limited range of colors from specialty stores and by mail order. Alternatively, buy clear glaze (sometimes called scumble glaze), and color it with universal tint or artist's oil paints. This is available from art stores. To paint a small room, you'll need about 1 pint (½ liter) of glaze. Use glaze over an oil-based base coat.

Emulsion. This can be thinned with water to make a glaze. This can be used for sponging, but it gives a flatter, harder, less attractive finish than glaze

or thinned oil-based paint. It dries too quickly to be used for dragging. Use thinned emulsion over a water-based base coat, such as vinyl silk.

Oil-based paint. This can be thinned with mineral spirits and used to make a soft glaze. It dries faster than glaze, so you'll have to work quickly. Use thinned oil paint over an oil-based base coat.

Tinting a glaze

If you can't get a ready-mixed glaze in the color you want, you can easily tint your own glaze. Mix enough for the whole room, keeping a note of the formula in case you need to mix up some more.

MATERIALS

Eggshell paint for base coat

Transparent oil glaze

Universal tint or artist's oil paint in your chosen color

mineral spirits

Spoon or cup for measuring

Paintbrush

Saucer

Paint kettle

White card

1 MIXING THE SHADE
Squeeze the tint or oil paint into the saucer. Add just enough mineral spirits to dissolve it, blending it with a paintbrush. Mix two colors together if required, keeping a note of their proportions. Spoon in a little transparent oil glaze and stir it in well, then test the color on the white card. The tone lightens when you add the rest of the glaze and mineral spirits, and appears less intense when brushed out sparingly.

2 MIXING THE GLAZE
When you're satisfied with the color, transfer the glaze into the paint can, measuring it with a spoon or cup. A useful ratio is seven parts glaze to two parts tint. Mix in the color. The glaze is quite thick, so by mixing up to one part of mineral spirits to every two parts of tinted glaze you will make it go much further. Don't thin the glaze too much, or it may run.

3 TESTING THE GLAZE
Paint the white card in the base color and let it dry. Paint a little of the glaze on top to check the results.

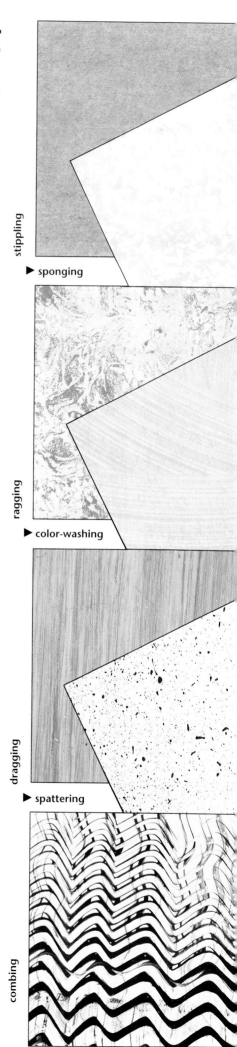

stippling

▶ sponging

ragging

▶ color-washing

dragging

▶ spattering

combing

STIPPLING

This broken-color technique creates a subtle, dappled texture, giving the base color greater depth. First, brush a tinted glaze over the base coat, and then dab it with the tip of a brush to break up the color. It's essential to use a tinted glaze for the top coat, because thinned paint dries too quickly.

Stippling looks best with a medium or dark glaze over an eggshell base coat in a paler shade of the same color.

For the best results, use stippling brushes made of fine bristles, available from art stores. These produce a fine effect that adds depth rather than pattern to the finished color. These brushes are expensive, but cheaper, plastic alternatives are now available. Or you can improvise by using a rough brush, such as a dustpan brush.

MATERIALS

Eggshell paint for the base coat

Tinted glaze for the top coat

Roller or decorator's brush to apply the base coat

Soft brush or clean cloth to apply the glaze

Stippling brush

Rubber gloves

Scrap paper or rags

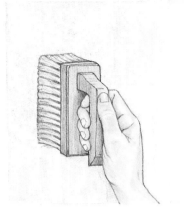

1 PAINTING THE BASE COAT
Make sure the surface is smooth and sound, then paint it with one or two coats of eggshell paint. Let it dry thoroughly.

2 APPLYING THE GLAZE
Using a soft brush or cloth, apply the tinted glaze to the base coat over a workable area. On a wall, cover a strip 1-2ft (30-60cm) wide.

3 STIPPLING THE GLAZE
Work quickly, while the glaze is wet. Starting at the top, press the stippling brush into the glaze. Maintain even pressure, and do not press too hard. When the brush gets soaked with paint, wipe it on rags or paper. Try not to break off in the middle of an area or the edge may show up as a ridge.

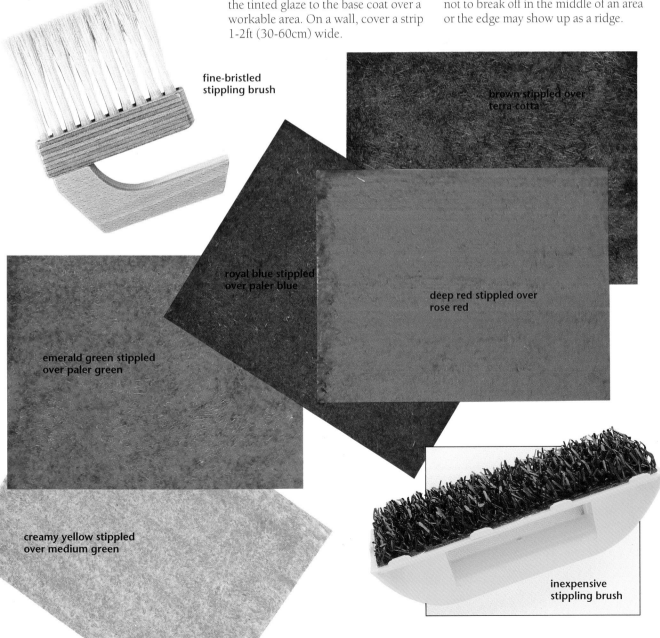

fine-bristled stippling brush

brown stippled over terra-cotta

royal blue stippled over paler blue

deep red stippled over rose red

emerald green stippled over paler green

creamy yellow stippled over medium green

inexpensive stippling brush

SPONGING

This is a popular broken-color technique that creates a mottled pattern, like soft clouds. All you do is paint the surface with a base coat and then dab over it with a sponge dipped in thinned paint or glaze in a second color. For added depth, you can sponge over it again in a third color, or even a fourth. Usually the base coat is paler than the sponged colors.

Natural sponges are best for sponge effects because they create an uneven, mottled pattern. You can use synthetic sponges, although they create a more regular pattern. Experiment with different types of sponges, like car sponges. The coarser the sponge, the rougher the effect.

MATERIALS

Paint for the base coat

Tinted glaze or thinned paint (add water/mineral spirits slowly until the paint is thin but not too runny) in one or more colors for the top coat

Paintbrush or roller to apply the base coat

Sponge to apply the top coat

Shallow dish or saucer

Rubber gloves

Scrap paper

---

1 PAINTING THE BASE COAT
Make sure the surface to be painted is smooth and sound. Prime it if necessary. Using the paintbrush or roller, apply one or two coats of the base color and let it dry.

SYNTHETIC SPONGES

With a synthetic sponge, you'll get a softer paint effect if you use the rounded edges only. Cut the sponge into handy sections to make this easier.

2 SPONGING THE FIRST COLOR
Wearing rubber gloves, pour a little thinned paint or glaze into the shallow dish or saucer. If you are using glaze, dip the sponge in mineral spirits and squeeze it out. Dip the sponge in the glaze or thinned paint and squeeze out the excess, then dab it on scrap paper to remove a bit more paint. Dab the sponge over the surface at random to leave a light, speckled pattern. If you are using just one top coat, keep the marks close together; if you are going to add another color, space out the marks. Continue sponging in this way.

3 CHECKING YOUR PROGRESS
Stand back every so often to check the effect. If you have sponged too heavily, you can sponge over this area later with the base color. If the effect is too light, go over it again with the top color.

4 APPLYING THE NEXT COLOR
Once the first sponged color is dry, you can sponge on a second color in the same way. Fill in some of the gaps between the first sponged layer and the base coat, and partially overlap the first sponged layer for a soft, blended look.

RAGGING

One of the simplest broken-color techniques is ragging. This is worked using rags to create patterns in thinned paint or glaze. It's quick to do and looks great on large areas like walls.

Different fabrics create slightly different patterns: the rougher the fabric, the stronger the pattern will be. Use old sheets for a smooth pattern, or try well-washed burlap or cheesecloth for a stronger design. You can even use paper or plastic bags. You'll need a large supply of rags, since they soon get soaked with paint.

Ragging methods

There are three basic ragging methods: ragging on, ragging off, and rag rolling. When ragging on, you use a rag dipped in glaze to create the pattern over the base coat. This produces a strong pattern that is easy to control. When ragging off, you paint the glaze over the base coat and then remove some with a dry rag. This produces a subtler pattern than ragging on.

The way you scrunch the rag will affect the type of pattern you create: the tighter the bundle, the more dense the pattern will be. If you like, you can roughly bunch the rag into a sausage shape and roll it over the surface to create an even pattern. This method is called rag rolling.

MATERIALS

Paint for the base coat

Thinned paint (add water/ mineral spirits slowly until the paint is thin but not too runny) or tinted glaze for the top coat

Roller or paintbrush to apply the base coat

Cloth or paintbrush to apply the top coat

Rags

Shallow dish or saucer

Rubber gloves

Scrap paper

RAGGING ON

Using the paintbrush or roller, apply one or two coats of the base color and let it dry.

Pour a little tinted glaze or thinned paint into the shallow dish or saucer. Wearing rubber gloves, scrunch a rag into a loose pad and dip it into the tinted glaze or thinned paint. Squeeze it out, then dab it over the painted surface. Vary the direction of the dabbing and refold the rag at intervals to create an irregular pattern. When the rag gets clogged with paint, rinse it in water or mineral spirits or change it for a fresh one.

RAGGING OFF

Apply the base coat as for RAGGING ON, and let it dry. Pour a little tinted glaze or thinned paint into the dish or saucer. Apply the glaze or thinned paint over the base coat with a cloth or paintbrush. Wearing rubber gloves, scrunch a rag into a loose pad, then press it lightly and quickly over the wet glaze. Keep changing the direction of your hand as you work and refold the rag at intervals to create an irregular pattern. Rinse or change the rag as necessary.

RAG ROLLING

Apply the base coat as for RAGGING ON, and let it dry. Apply the glaze or thinned paint over the base coat with a cloth or paintbrush. Bunch a rag into a sausage shape and lightly roll it over the surface in an irregular, meandering line. When working on a wall, work from the bottom up. When you start the next roll, just overlap the previous roll line to blend over the join. Take care not to skid over the surface of the glaze as you roll.

PATCHING UP

Stand back every now and then to judge your work. If you've missed a patch, touch it up lightly with a rag. If there's an area that has too much glaze, rub it off with a rag dampened with mineral spirits or water, and immediately glaze and rag over it again, blending it in.

If the ragged pattern is too distinct, let it dry for half an hour, then dab over it with the tip of a paintbrush. This will blur the edges, creating a softer effect.

COLOR-WASHING

This paint effect is accomplished by brushing colored glaze or highly diluted paint over a base coat, so that the base color shows through. The brushmarks are often visible, which gives an informal, cottage look. Color-washing looks good on large areas like walls and helps to disguise rough plaster. It's also a useful way to adjust a color you're disappointed with.

Pale shades are especially suited to this technique, but you can use it with stronger colors – because the wash is so thin, the effect won't be too dark.

Materials

Paint. For the best results, use eggshell paint for the base coat and use oil-based scumble glaze mixed with eggshell paint and mineral spirits for the color wash (see below). This mixture has a fairly thick consistency, so it won't run down the wall, and when it's finished the color wash will have an attractive, translucent look. Oil-based scumble glaze is available from art and decorating stores.

Alternatively, use emulsion paint for the base coat and heavily diluted emulsion paint for the color wash (see opposite). Diluted emulsion is very runny, so it can be messy to handle. The finished effect is similar to old-fashioned whitewash.

Brushes. Use a 4in (100mm) decorator's brush to apply the color wash. You'll also need a dry brush to soften the color. Alternatively, you can use a dragging brush or a specialist graining brush to give a more textured finish. You can also apply the color wash with an old rag.

Color-washing with glaze

This technique is easier than color-washing with emulsion paint, since the glaze is less likely to run.

MATERIALS

Eggshell paint for the base coat

Eggshell paint for the color wash

Scumble glaze

mineral spirits

Decorator's brush or roller to apply the base coat

Two 4in (100mm) decorator's brushes with long, flexible bristles

Container for mixing the glaze

Old rags

1 APPLYING THE BASE COAT
Make sure the surface is smooth and sound, then paint it with one or two coats of the eggshell base color. Let it dry thoroughly.

2 MIXING THE GLAZE
In the container, mix five parts of eggshell paint with three parts scumble glaze and two parts mineral spirits. Stir the mixture well to blend it thoroughly.

3 APPLYING THE GLAZE
Using one of the 4in (100mm) decorator's brushes, apply the glaze solution with loose, random strokes.

4 SOFTENING THE STROKES
While the glaze is still wet, use a dry brush to go over the surface with light, random strokes to remove some of the paint and to soften the brush marks. Wipe the brush frequently with old rags to remove excess paint. If you like, repeat this step for a mellow finish.

Color-washing with emulsion

Emulsion dries quickly, so when you're applying the top coat, either work on a small area at a time or ask a friend to help.

MATERIALS

Emulsion paint for the base coat

Emulsion paint for the color wash

Container to mix the paint

Roller or paintbrush

Two 4in (100mm) brushes

Old rags

1 APPLYING THE BASE COAT
Make sure that the surface is smooth and sound, then paint it with one or two coats of the base color. Let it dry thoroughly.

2 APPLYING THE WASH
In the container, dilute the emulsion for the top coat with water: use one part paint to at least four parts water. Using the 4in (100mm) paintbrush and large, vigorous strokes, apply the wash over the base coat.

3 SOFTENING THE STROKES
Before the color wash dries, use a dry brush to soften the brush strokes. Wipe the brush frequently with old rags to remove excess paint. If you like, repeat this step for a mellow finish.

COLOR-RUBBING

Color-rubbing gives wood a soft patina and allows some of the grain to show through. Diluted paint is simply rubbed into the wood, then the surface is protected with varnish.

Test the paint first on a hidden area. The color should penetrate the wood without obscuring the grain.

MATERIALS

Emulsion or oil-based paint and mineral spirits

Container to mix the paint

Household paintbrush

Medium and fine-grade sandpaper and a sanding block

Lint-free rags

Polyurethane varnish and a varnish brush

1 APPLYING THE PAINT
Strip off any finishes and prepare the wood for painting. Pour the paint into the container and thin it slightly: use mineral spirits for oil-based paint and water for water-based paint.

Paint a small area of the wood, applying the paint in the direction of the grain. Using a rag, rub the paint into the surface. Repeat until the whole area is covered, discarding the rags when they are saturated with paint.

2 MAKING THE COLOR DEEPER
For a deeper color, apply more paint in the same way. If you want more of the wood grain to show through, rub over the wood with a rag dampened with mineral spirits or water.

3 DISTRESSING (OPTIONAL)
For a distressed effect, use fine sandpaper to remove a little color, working in the direction of the grain.

4 FINISHING OFF
When the paint is dry, brush on a thin layer of varnish. If the item will get heavy wear, apply two or more coats of varnish. Floorboards need at least three coats.

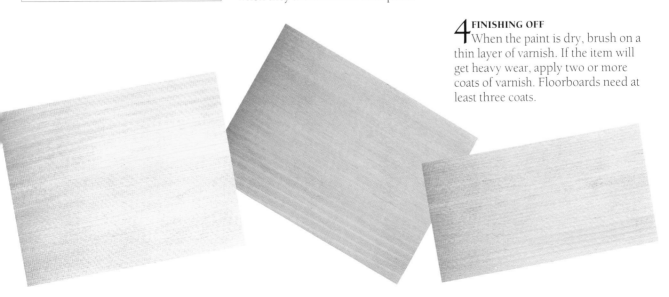

MARBLING

Beautiful but expensive, marble is a stone that many people admire. You can achieve a similar effect with paint and glaze. Just paint the surface in a background color, mottle it with a glaze, and add veins in two or more colors. It's easier to copy marble rather than trying to create a pattern yourself. Look at the painted samples here; use pictures of real marble in catalogs, books, or magazines.

PLANNING THE EFFECT

Before you start, practice the marbling technique on a piece of board. When you're confident with the effect, paint a small item that could be made from real marble: tabletops, bath panels, or fireplace surrounds are all good projects for beginners.

MATERIALS

Oil-based eggshell. Use this for the base coat. You can use water-based paint, but you'll get more realistic results with oil-based paint. Generally the base coat is lighter than the glaze.

Glaze. Use scumble glaze, which is a beige, jellylike substance that dries clear. It can be tinted to create a film of color through which you can see the base color. Scumble glaze can be either oil-based or acrylic. Both types are available from art and decorating stores, and you can buy ready-tinted glaze in a few colors.

Oil-based scumble glaze is slow drying, so it's easy to use, and it can be tinted with artist's oil paints or universal tints. After a while, it will yellow slightly, so it's unsuitable for white marble. However, it gives colored marble an attractive antiqued look.

Acrylic scumble glaze dries more quickly than oil-based glaze, so you have to work fast. It doesn't turn yellow, so it's the best choice for white marble effects. Tint this type of scumble glaze with artist's acrylic paint.

Color. To create realistic shading, use two or three shades of glaze. For oil-based scumble glaze, use *artist's oil paints* to tint the glaze and to paint in the veins. Tint acrylic scumble glaze with *artist's acrylic paints* instead. You can also use *universal tints*.

Thinner. Thin oil-based glaze with *mineral spirits*. Use *water* for thinning acrylic glaze.

Varnish. Use a medium-sheen acrylic or polyurethane varnish. Choose polyurethane varnish for surfaces that will get a lot of wear. You'll need at least two to five coats.

Paintbrushes. You'll need a ½-1in (12-25mm) household brush for applying the base coat, glazes, and varnish, and at least one fine, round, or flat artist's brush for the veining. A 2in (50mm) hogshair brush is useful for softening the veins, but, for small areas, you could use a sponge instead.

Cloths or sponges. These are used to soften the glazes. Lint-free cloths and natural sponges are best.

Feathers. These can be used instead of artist's brushes for the veining, but they are difficult to use and quickly become clogged with paint.

▶ *These marble samples were painted with a base color, two glazes, and two veining colors.*

Green marble: medium green base coat; a glaze of viridian plus burnt umber and of viridian plus Prussian blue plus black; veining in white and in black. Adjust proportions as required.

Ocher marble: pale yellow base coat; glazes in ocher plus white and in ocher plus raw umber plus white; veining in raw sienna and in raw umber.

Black marble: black base coat; glazes in white and in Payne's gray plus white; veining in black and white.

Pink marble: pale pink base coat; glazes in Indian red plus ocher plus white and in crimson red plus ocher plus white; veining in Indian red and in raw umber.

White/gray marble: white base coat; glazes in Payne's gray plus white and in Davy's gray plus white; veining in Payne's gray and in black.

▲ green marble

ocher marble

▲ black marble

pink marble

white/gray marble

◀ green marble

Marbling a surface

There are many recipes for decorative glazes and many methods of applying them. The instructions given here should be used just as a guide.

MATERIALS

Eggshell paint in your base color

Oil or acrylic scumble glaze

Artist's oil paint to tint oil-based glaze, or acrylic paint to tint acrylic glaze in white plus at least two other colors

Thinner: mineral spirits or water

Two ½-1in (12-25mm) paintbrushes

Fine, round, or flat artist's brush

Lint-free cloths

Natural sponge (optional)

Hogshair softening brush or other very soft brush

Fine sandpaper

Three glass jars

Old white plate

Old spoon

Rubber gloves

3 APPLYING THE GLAZES
Use a rag to rub full-strength scumble glaze over the surface. Use a paintbrush to apply the palest glaze roughly over some areas. Then apply the medium colored glaze over other areas, leaving the base coat exposed in a few places. Quickly press a bunched-up rag or a sponge over the surface to remove the glaze from some areas and soften others.

4 SOFTENING THE EFFECT
Glide the hogshair brush over the surface, working diagonally from the top left to the bottom right and then from the top right to the bottom left, working the colors in well.

6 ADDING MORE VEINS
Soften the veins diagonally with the hogshair brush. Add sharp veins of darker and lighter tones with the artist's brush and paint diluted with thinner. These new veins can cross and blend with the previously painted veins, but should not be softened.

7 LIFTING OFF COLOR
By now the background color will be almost completely covered up. To bring areas back to the base color, cover a gloved finger with a rag, dip it into mineral spirits and press it onto the surface. This will lift out tiny islands of color. Cotton-wool buds can also be used to lift out smaller areas of color.

8 VARNISHING THE SURFACE
Apply two or more coats of varnish with your second household paintbrush, lightly sanding between the coats. Let the surface dry.

1 PAINTING THE BASE COAT
Prepare the surface to be painted, and prime it if necessary. The surface should be as smooth as possible. Apply two coats of eggshell paint, sanding lightly after each coat. Let the paint dry.

2 MAKING THE GLAZE
Make three glazes in different shades of the same color. To do this, squeeze some of your medium color artist's oil paint onto the white plate; mix it with other colors to get exactly the shade you want. Add a little glaze and thinner to create a creamy texture. Put a spoonful of the color into each jar. Add a little white or pale paint to one jar to make the lighter shade, and a little darker paint into another jar. Add seven to fourteen spoons of scumble glaze to each jar and a dash of thinner, mixing them thoroughly. Make sure you have enough of each glaze to cover the whole surface.

5 ADDING THE SHADOW VEINS
Starting at the top, use the artist's brush and darkest glaze to create a random, diagonal pattern of veins. Keep the veins 2-4in (5-10cm) apart, and split them into groups of two or three at intervals.

IF THINGS GO WRONG

Brush marks can mean you've applied too much full-strength scumble glaze at the beginning. Either wipe off the glazes and start again, applying less glaze, or take off some of the glaze with a dry hogshair brush and continue marbling.

The brush won't glide over the surface smoothly if you haven't used enough full-strength glaze or if the tinted glaze is too thick. Wipe off the tinted glaze and add more undiluted glaze, or thin the tinted glaze.

DRAGGING

This broken-color paint technique gives surfaces a simple wood-grain effect. It looks elegant on walls, but since it's one of the most difficult paint techniques to master, especially over a large area, it's sensible to practice first on smaller surfaces, such as furniture and doors.

Dragging is worked by applying a tinted glaze over the base coat and then dragging a long-bristled, dry brush over the surface with long, straight strokes, so that very narrow stripes of the base color show through. It's advisable to use glaze for the top coat, since thinned paint dries too quickly for the effect to work properly.

Dragging works to its best effect when the dragged color is darker than the base coat: use a deeper tone of the base color, or a color over white or cream.

Professional dragging brushes (also known as flogging brushes) have long, flexible bristles. They produce the best dragged finishes, but they're very expensive. For woodwork, you could substitute an ordinary paintbrush or a varnish brush; for walls, use a wide paper-hanging brush.

MATERIALS

Eggshell paint for the base coat

Tinted glaze for the top coat

Clear matte or semigloss varnish (optional)

Paintbrush or roller to apply the base coat

Soft brush to apply the glaze

Dragging or flogging brush

Paint can or roller tray

Rubber gloves (optional)

Rags

Shallow dish or saucer

Mineral spirits

Plumb line and chalk (optional)

1 PAINTING THE BASE COAT
Make sure the surface to be painted is smooth and sound. Prime it, if necessary. Using the paintbrush or roller, apply one or two coats of the base color, and let it dry thoroughly.

3 DRAGGING THE GLAZE
Working quickly, while the glaze is still wet, drag the dry dragging brush down the surface. Work firmly to achieve bold, straight lines that reveal the base color. Repeat this action, with the next strokes parallel to and slightly overlapping the first ones. When the brush gets soaked with paint, wipe it clean with a rag soaked in mineral spirits.

DRAGGING WALLS
Work with a partner: one of you can apply the glaze while the other does the dragging.

To help to guide your brush, start near a natural vertical, such as a door frame. Alternatively, mark vertical guidelines on the wall using a plumb line and chalk. Start at the top of the wall, dragging the brush downward. If the room is too high to drag the wall in one stroke, feather the joins together.

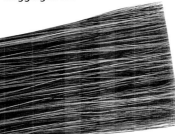

flogging brush

2 APPLYING THE GLAZE
Using the soft brush, apply the tinted glaze over a workable area. If you are working on a wall, cover a strip about 1½-2ft (46-60cm) wide.

DRAGGING WOOD
Follow the direction of the grain. Allow each section to dry completely before starting on the next section. Let the dragged glaze dry thoroughly for at least two days, then protect the surface with at least two coats of clear matte or semigloss varnish.

▼ *Orange dragged over pale orange*

▼ *Medium blue dragged over pale blue*

COMBING

This technique gives surfaces a much bolder, coarser effect than dragging. It's easier than dragging, and you can use it to create a variety of patterns, such as stripes, diagonals, crosses, and waves.

Combing is accomplished by brushing tinted glaze or thinned oil-based paint over the base coat and then combing it while the glaze is still wet, so that the base coat shows through. The top coat should be thick enough to hold the texture of the combing.

For the best effect, the top coat should contrast with the base coat. For example, comb a medium-colored glaze over a white or pale-colored base, or use a dark base under a medium-colored glaze.

Wood-graining combs are usually made of rubber and come in a range of sizes. Some have graduated teeth that produce a series of lines with varying widths and spaces. You can make your own comb from plywood or cardboard, or adapt an Afro comb or a tile adhesive spreader.

MATERIALS

Eggshell paint for the base coat

Tinted glaze or thinned oil-based paint (add up to 25 percent mineral spirits, stirring it in slowly) for the top coat

Clear matte or semigloss varnish (optional)

Paintbrush or roller to apply the base coat

Soft brush to apply the top coat

Comb

Rags

Paint can or roller tray

Mineral spirits

Rubber gloves (optional)

Scrap paper

1 PAINTING THE BASE COAT
Make sure the surface to be painted is smooth and sound. Prime it, if necessary. Using the paintbrush or roller, apply one or two coats of the base color and let it dry thoroughly.

2 APPLYING THE GLAZE
Using the soft brush, apply the tinted glaze over a workable area. If you are working on a wall, cover a strip about 1½-2ft (46-60cm) wide.

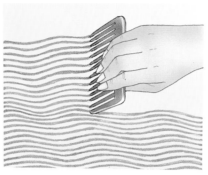

3 COMBING THE TOP COAT
Keeping your strokes as even as possible, drag the comb firmly through the wet surface to reveal the contrasting color of the base coat beneath. If you like, vary the pattern by changing the direction of the strokes. If the comb becomes clogged with paint, wipe it clean with a rag dipped in mineral spirits.

4 FINISHING OFF
Let the paint dry thoroughly. If you have used glaze, this may take up to two days. If the combed area will receive a lot of wear and tear, protect it with at least two coats of clear matte or semigloss varnish.

combing tools

▲ *Diagonal crosses in green over cream*

▲ *Swirly pattern in red over blue*

▲ *Criss-cross pattern in blue over yellow*

PAINTING WALLS AND CEILINGS

A new coat of paint is often all that's needed to refresh interior decorations. With a friend to help, you can paint the ceiling and walls of a medium-sized room in a day. If you're working alone, make sure you've got time to finish a whole ceiling or wall in one session; a dried paint edge may show up as a line.

Choosing paint

Most painting is done with emulsion paint, but for special effects and particular problems, you may need to use a special type of paint. See OTHER PAINT, below, for further details.

EMULSION PAINT

This water-based paint is the best finish for walls and ceilings. It is easy to apply to large areas, dries quickly, and wears well. One coat should cover 14-17sq yd (12-14sq m) per 1/4 gallon (liter), depending on how porous the surface is. Check the details on the can for precise information.

Solid emulsion. Quick to apply and drip-free, this is a good choice for ceilings. However, it comes in a limited range of colors and it's more expensive than ordinary paint.

Vinyl matte. This provides a smooth, matte finish. It has no shine, so it won't show up slight irregularities on the surface of the walls or ceiling. Use a roller with a long-pile sleeve.

Vinyl silk. This has a soft sheen that looks good on smooth surfaces, textured lining papers, and paneled walls. It is more durable than matte, but it may show up irregularities on the surface of the wall or ceiling. Use a roller with a short-pile sleeve.

OTHER PAINT

Eggshell. An oil-based paint, this is often used for kitchens and bathrooms because it resists condensation. You can also use special emulsion paint, which has a high acrylic content, for these areas.

Textured paint. This is a thick paint that can be used to create a thick texture or pattern. It's also useful for covering small cracks and other minor defects. Apply it with a brush, roller, or a texturing tool such as a comb, sponge, or stippling brush.

Primer. This should be used on bare plaster walls and ceilings before they are painted. Use latex rather than oil-based primers, because they are easy to use and quick-drying.

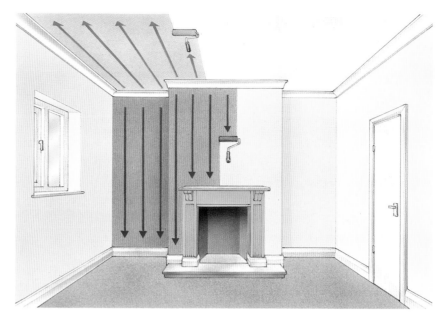

Painting a room

If the walls and ceiling are bare, prime them first. Then paint the ceiling, then the walls, then cornices, and finally any woodwork and radiators.

Ceilings. Start by painting a narrow margin around the edges and corners. Then work in broad, parallel strips away from the light of the window.

Walls. With a small brush, paint along the edges of baseboards, behind radiators, and around the window frames and light switches, etc. Start at the window wall, at the top right-hand corner (top left if left-handed), and work away from the light. When using emulsion paint, work in horizontal bands from the ceiling downward.

Cornices. If you are painting the cornice a contrasting color, paint it next.

Woodwork. Paint woodwork and radiators with gloss or satin paint.

MATERIALS

Paint

Roller or large paintbrush

Small paintbrush

Sealer, if the surface is stained with watermarks

Protective sheets

Old newspapers

Masking tape

Old rags

Roller tray (optional)

Working platform (e.g., two step ladders and a plank of wood)

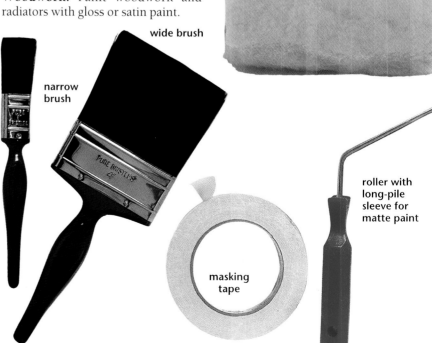

wide brush

narrow brush

masking tape

roller with long-pile sleeve for matte paint

GETTING STARTED

1 PREPARING THE ROOM
Prepare the walls for painting. Remove as much furniture as possible; move the rest to the center of the room and cover it with protective sheets. Cover the floor with old newspapers.

2 PAINTING BEHIND RADIATORS
Turn off the radiators so that paint splashes do not dry hard before you can wipe them off. Paint as far behind them as you can with a small brush or a radiator roller.

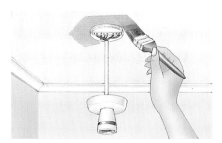

3 PAINTING AROUND SOCKETS
For sockets, switches, and light fixtures, turn off the electricity first, then loosen the screws so the cover plate comes away and you can get the brush just underneath it. Unscrew the cover on a ceiling fixture.

REMOVING WATER STAINS
If water has stained the ceiling at some time, paint the area with sealer; otherwise, the stain will show through the new paint.

REMOVING NICOTINE STAINS
If the ceiling or walls are stained with nicotine, try to clean off as much as possible with degreaser or a washing-soda solution. Let the area dry. Coat the ceiling with sealer, diluting it as instructed on the can. Let the sealer dry, then paint the area with two coats of paint.

PAINTING WITH A ROLLER
A roller applies paint thicker and quicker than a brush, but you will need to paint the edges and awkward corners of the surface first, since a roller can't get into these areas. Two coats of paint should be sufficient unless the color underneath was much darker or unless the surface is very porous.

LABOR SAVER

There's no need to clean the roller and tray between painting sessions done on the same day. Just pour off the paint and put the equipment in a plastic bag to prevent it from drying out. Wrap wet brushes in plastic wrap.

PAINTING WITH A BRUSH
Use a brush for painting the edges of large areas, for awkward corners and small areas, and when using runny paint, such as some eggshell paints. Unless you are recoating a wall in the same color or one that is very similar, you will probably need to apply two or three coats of paint.

1 COATING THE ROLLER
Pour enough paint into the tray to fill the deep end only. Dip the roller lightly into the paint, then roll it on the ribbed surface until it is evenly coated. If it drips when you lift it up, roll a bit off.

2 USING THE ROLLER
Push the roller gently along the ceiling or wall in zigzag strokes, covering the surface in all directions. Finish by rollering up and down to ensure the paint is even.

USING A BRUSH
Paint the edges of the walls and ceiling with a small brush. Change to a 4in (100mm) brush and paint in horizontal strokes. Brush over the area with vertical strokes for even coverage.

Safety first

When painting high areas, always work from a stepladder rather than a chair, so that you have a platform to put the paint on and a support to hold onto. Paint only where you can reach comfortably without stretching out too far. On ceilings, paint the area in front of you, not directly over your head, so you don't get splashed.

If you are painting a stairwell, try using a special roller with an extension handle so you can reach the upper parts. Alternatively, construct a platform using two ladders and a stout scaffold board.

Cleaning up

Clean your equipment immediately, following the paint manufacturer's instructions. Clean off latex-based paints under running water until not a trace of paint comes out. Use mineral spirits to clean off oil-based paint.

Leave the brushes or rollers to dry, then store them flat in a plastic bag to keep out dust.

Leftover paint. This can be resealed in the can: Press the lid down firmly and then turn the can upside down, so that the paint seals the lid. If there is just a little paint left, store it in a large, clean, screw-top jar, labeled with the name and serial number of the paint. Keep all leftover emulsion paint in a frost-free place; frost ruins emulsion.

BASIC TILING

With the right tools and careful planning and preparation, even a beginner can tile a surface successfully. You can use this guide to tile any flat surface, but if you've never done tiling before, start with a small, simple project, such as a splashback in a kitchen or bathroom.

TILE CHOICE

Ceramic tiles provide a long-lasting, hardwearing surface that is decorative and easy to clean. Matte, semimatte, or gloss finishes are available in a wide range of colors. Some patterned tiles have a complete design on each tile, others a design that is split over two or more tiles. Border tiles are sold in complementary colors.

Most tiles are rectangular or square, but you can also buy hexagonal ones. The majority of tiles have square edges, but round-edged ones, better for exposed ends, are also available; and you can get tiles that have edgings specially shaped for countertops. Some tiles have spacer lugs that

sealant
and spreader

tile nibblers

tile spacers

tile
cutter

ensure equal joints between each tile; if yours don't, use plastic spacers or matchsticks to space them evenly.

CALCULATING QUANTITIES

Measure the area to be tiled. Divide this area by the size of one tile to give you the exact number of tiles required, then add at least 10 percent extra for breakage and cutting.

MATERIALS

Tiles

Tiling adhesive and spreader

Grout

Silicone sealant or PVC seal strip

Tile spacers or matchsticks

1⅜ yd (1.25m) length of narrow timber

Two wooden battens

Hammer and nails

Squeegee and sponge

Carpenter's level

Metal ruler, pen or pencil

Retractable tape measure

Round-tipped stick or blunt pencil

Tile cutter, scorer and breaker

Tile file

Tile nibblers or pliers

Masonry nails and hammer

Wet-and-dry sandpaper

PREPARING THE WALL

The wall's surface must be smooth and sound. Strip off old wallpaper or lining paper, fill all the cracks and holes, and remove any flaking paint. Rub down gloss or semigloss paint with wet-and-dry sandpaper to give a proper surface for the adhesive.

Powdery or porous walls (especially new plaster). These should be brushed with a coat of stabilizing solution to provide a sound base; allow it to dry out completely before tiling the wall. New plaster should be allowed to dry out for at least four weeks before tiling it.

PLOTTING THE LAYOUT

1 PLANNING THE TILE POSITIONS
Place a row of tiles in front of the wall to find the best arrangement. A symmetrical arrangement usually looks best, with cut tiles at each end. Place whole tiles around focal points, such as windows, and work out from there.

2 USING THE GAUGING ROD
To make the gauging rod, mark off tile widths plus spacer widths on the 1⅜ yd (1.25m) length of timber. Holding the rod horizontally against the wall, plot the course of a whole row of tiles, adjusting it so that the cut tiles at the edges are of equal width. Mark the position of the bottom of the first whole tile on the wall. Repeat vertically, marking the left edge of the first tile.

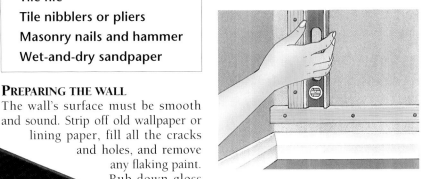

3 ATTACHING THE BATTENS
Battens provide an accurate tiling guide. Draw a horizontal line under the second marked row of tiles from the bottom. This marks the position of the horizontal batten. Use a carpenter's level to check that the line is horizontal, then nail on the batten, leaving the nail heads sticking up so that the nails can easily be removed later.

Fix a second batten up the left side of the wall, one tile in from the edge. Check that the batten is vertical with the level. Place a tile in the corner to check accuracy. Mark the battens with the tile and spacer positions.

GLUING ON THE TILES

The area inside the battens is tiled first and left to set for 12 hours, then the battens are removed and the bottom and side tiles are added.

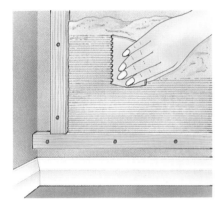

1 APPLYING THE ADHESIVE
Starting in the corner formed by the battens, use the notched spreader to apply tile adhesive. Work on an area the size of six tiles. Avoid getting adhesive on the batten.

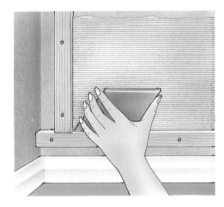

2 POSITIONING THE FIRST TILE
Rest the bottom edge of the tile on the batten, holding the tile at an angle of 45 degrees to the wall. Align the tile with the vertical batten and press the tile firmly into the adhesive. Check that it is level using the carpenter's level; if not, twist it slightly until it is.

3 ADDING TILES
Continue laying tiles along the row in the same way. If you're using standard tiles without molded-on spacer lugs, position tile spacers at the upper corners of each tile. The spacers can be removed after about an hour and used elsewhere.

Make sure the tiles lie flush with one another so that the final surface is smooth and flat. Press in any tiles that are sticking out. Remove any that have sunk too deep into the adhesive and put some more adhesive on the wall before re-bedding them.

4 FINISHING THE WHOLE TILES
Adhere the tiles over the remaining area, using the carpenter's level to check that they are straight. Wipe off any excess adhesive with a damp sponge.

5 TILING THE EDGES
To fill any gaps at the edges, place a tile in each gap, glazed side down, and mark it at the top and bottom with a marker pen; allow space for the grout. On the glazed side, join the marks with the pen and metal ruler. Check that the tile fits the gap before cutting it.

6 CUTTING THE TILES
Firmly score once along the marked line, using the metal ruler to guide the blade. Position the jaws of the snapping tool on either side of the marked line, and squeeze it to make a clean break. Smooth down the cut edges with a file before fixing the tile in place. If a tile only needs to be trimmed, score the tile, then use pliers or nibblers to remove the excess.

7 ADDING THE LAST TILES
When all the tiles have been laid, wipe them clean and allow 24 hours for the adhesive to set completely. If you are using battens, wait until the tiles are firmly fixed and the adhesive has set. Then you can remove the battens and tile the last row. Let the adhesive set thoroughly.

FINISHING OFF

Fill the gaps between the tiles with grout. This seals the tiles and gives them a neat finish. Grout is a cement-based paste that comes ready-mixed or in powder form for mixing with water and it is available in a wide range of colors. Special waterproof grouts are available for tiled areas in bathrooms and kitchens.

Narrow gaps between a bath or basin and a tiled wall should be filled with a flexible, watertight sealant rather than grout (see below).

1 APPLYING THE GROUT
If you are using grout powder, mix it to a thick paste according to the manufacturer's instructions. Using a rubber squeegee or sponge, force the grout between the tiles, filling the spaces tightly. Clean off any excess grout with a damp sponge before it dries.

2 PACKING THE GROUT
When the grout has hardened a little, run a stick with a round point or a blunt pencil between the tiles to pack in the grout and give it a curved finish.

SEALING THE EDGES
If you're tiling around a shower, bath, or sink, use a silicone sealant or PVC strip to seal the edges. To apply sealant, snip off the end of the nozzle. Press the applicator into the back of the tube to squeeze the sealant onto the wall. For a smooth finish, dampen your finger and run it over the sealant.

BASIC PAPER HANGING

Wallpaper adds color and texture to a room and will also disguise imperfections in a wall's surface. It's not difficult to hang wallpaper, if you work carefully. It's a good idea to ask a friend to help; one can work at the pasting table while the other hangs the wallpaper.

CHOOSING WALLPAPER

If you're a beginner, it's best to avoid wallpapers with a large pattern, since matching the pattern across a join can cause problems and any mistakes are very obvious. The easiest wallpaper to hang is a medium-priced paper of medium weight, either plain, textured, or with a small random pattern.

Vinyl is easy to hang if your walls are flat, since it does not stretch, but choose regular wallpaper for bumpy walls because it has more "give." Vinyl wallpaper takes a long time to dry, so unless it's a ready-pasted vinyl, use a paste that contains fungicide to avoid mold. Textured papers are useful for covering up bumpy walls. For kitchens and bathrooms, choose a washable paper to withstand damp conditions. For speed, buy ready-pasted paper. Avoid very inexpensive wallpapers, since they tend to tear easily.

Buy all the paper you need at the same time and check that all the rolls have the same lot number, since the color may vary slightly between lots. If your wallpaper has a large pattern, buy an extra roll to allow for pattern matching.

Lining paper. Use plain lining paper to improve uneven or cracked plasterwork and to provide a good, clean surface for new wallpaper. Use a light-grade lining paper under ordinary wallpaper and a heavier one for rough surfaces and textured wall coverings.

MATERIALS AND EQUIPMENT

Table. To mark up and paste lengths of wallpaper, you will need a table about 6ft 7in (2m) long. A folding pasting table is the ideal width, easy to move, and reasonably priced.

Size or sizing. This is used to prepare bare walls. Most wallpaper pastes can be diluted with water to make a size, following the manufacturer's instructions.

Wallpaper paste. This is usually sold as powder or flakes. Use wallpaper paste for ordinary paper, and paste containing fungicide for vinyl and other washable wallpapers. Follow the manufacturer's mixing instructions and let the paste stand for the time given. Heavyweight wall coverings need special heavy-duty paste.

Plastic bucket. Use a bucket for mixing paste with a wooden spoon or stick for blending.

Pasting brush. An old 4in (100mm) paintbrush is ideal for applying paste.

Paper-hanging brush. A brush with soft bristles is best for smoothing the paper onto the wall. Make sure that the brush is clean and dry, because any paste splashes on the right side of the paper will leave a mark. For washable papers, use a dry sponge instead.

Measuring tape. For accuracy, use a metal tape measure to measure wall heights and lengths of paper.

Plumb bob and line. These are essential for establishing a vertical so that you hang the wallpaper in a straight line. You can use any small weight attached to a piece of cord.

Scissors. Use long-bladed scissors for cutting lengths. Use short-bladed scissors or a craft knife for trimming.

Seam roller. This is a very useful tool for smoothing the edges of lengths of paper firmly to the wall. Do not use a seam roller on embossed papers.

Sponge. Use a sponge or plenty of rags for cleaning up any blobs of paste.

Stepladder. Use a stepladder to help you reach the top of the wall comfortably. For a firmer footing, use two stepladders and a plank.

Other useful items. These include *clips* to hold the paper on the table, a *cutting guide* to help you cut each length accurately, and a *roll holder* to secure the roll of paper on the table.

CALCULATING QUANTITIES

Measure the height of the room from the floor or baseboard to cornice or ceiling – this is the length, or "drop." Then measure the distance around the walls. Don't deduct the space taken up by doors and windows. Use these measurements to calculate how many rolls you need, using the chart below. The measurement of a standard roll of wallpaper is approximately 33ft (10m) long and 2in (53cm) wide.

HOW MANY ROLLS?

Distance around walls	feet	33	36	39	43	46	49	52	56	59	62	66	69
	meters	10	11	12	13	14	15	16	17	18	19	20	21
Drop length						Number of rolls needed							
6ft 6in–7ft 2in	(2–2.2m)	5	5	5	6	6	7	7	7	8	8	9	9
7ft 2in–7ft 10in	(2.2–2.4m)	5	5	6	6	7	8	8	8	9	9	10	10
7ft 10in–8ft 6in	(2.4–2.6m)	5	6	6	7	7	8	8	9	9	10	10	11
8ft 6in–9ft 2in	(2.6–2.8m)	6	6	7	7	8	8	9	9	10	11	11	12
9ft 2in–9ft 10in	(2.8–3m)	6	7	7	8	8	9	9	10	11	11	12	12
9ft 10in–10ft 6in	(3–3.2m)	6	7	8	8	9	10	10	11	11	12	13	13
10ft 6in–11ft 2in	(3.2–3.4m)	7	7	8	9	9	10	11	11	12	13	13	14

PREPARATION

The surface to be papered should be as clean and smooth as possible. Remove old wall coverings and rinse off any remaining adhesive. Seal new plaster with a thin coat of size. Apply the size with an old paintbrush, and wipe off any drips as you go with a damp cloth.

LINING PAPER

If you are using lining paper under wallpaper, hang it horizontally (across the wall) so that you don't have two layers of vertical joins. Use the same paste as you will use for the final wall covering.

Start at ceiling level and work down, butting the joins closely. Let the lining paper dry for 24 hours. If the edges do overlap, rub them down lightly with medium-grade sandpaper.

TO START

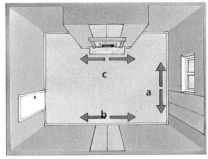

ORDER OF WORK

Traditionally, the edges of wallpaper overlapped, so wallpaper was hung starting beside the largest window and working away from it in both directions, so that any shadows cast at the joins didn't show (**a**). Nowadays, however, nearly all wallpapers are designed so that the drops simply butt together instead of overlapping; this means that you can start hanging the wallpaper on whichever wall gives you a long unobstructed run. Start at the center of the wall and work toward the edges (**b**). Never start in a corner of the room, since the corners may not be exactly square.

If you are using a wallpaper with a *large, bold pattern*, the first drop should be centered on a focal point, such as a chimney (**c**). Then work outward in both directions.

If you are working with a wallpaper with *large motifs*, position the wallpaper so that there is a complete motif at the top of the wall, where it will be most obvious.

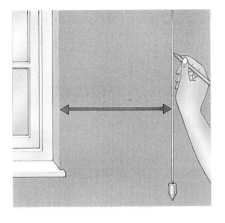

1 FINDING A VERTICAL

Use a plumb line and pencil to mark a vertical line down the length of the wall. You will hang the first length of paper against this line to ensure that the wallpaper is hung absolutely straight. When working on a wall with a window or door, measure out from the frame a distance of ¾in (20mm) less than the width of your paper. Then mark the vertical line here.

2 MEASURING THE DROP

Measure the height of the wall and add on 4in (10cm) to allow for trimming at the top and bottom. This measurement can be used for all the full lengths of paper. Lay the wallpaper face up on the pasting table and measure out the first length. Decide where the pattern will be placed. If the paper has a dominant print, make sure that a full pattern repeat is at the top of the wall, where it is most obvious.

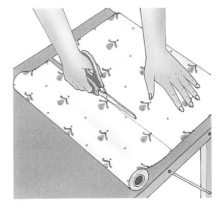

3 CUTTING THE DROP

Lightly mark the cutting line in pencil across the paper, making sure that it is at right angles to the edges. Cut the paper along the line with longbladed scissors.

◄ *Labor-saving devices for wallpapering can be bought from large home furnishing centers.*

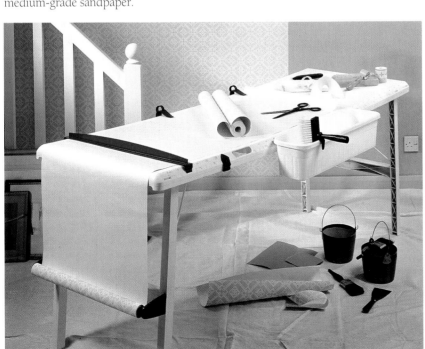

PASTING THE PAPER

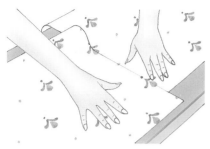

1 MATCHING THE PATTERN
Check the next length of paper against your first piece to match the pattern before cutting it. Cut four to five lengths, matching the pattern. Mark the top of each length on the back to avoid hanging patterns upside down, and number the lengths as you cut them. Keep short pieces for filling in over doors and windows.

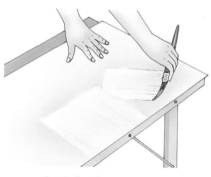

2 STARTING TO PASTE
Lay the first length face down on the table. Align the top end of the paper with the end of the table and have one long edge of the paper fractionally overlapping the side of the table farthest from you.

Start pasting from the center, working outward and away from you, and spread the paste evenly right up to the far edges. Covering the edges is most important, but always brush from the center outward. This is in order to avoid getting paste on the patterned side.

Move the paper toward you so that the paper overlaps the front edge of the table, and brush toward you to get a good covering of paste on the remaining edges.

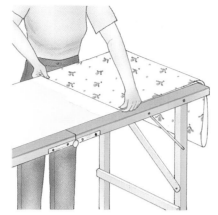

3 FINISHING AND FOLDING
Fold the pasted section neatly in half with the pasted sides together. Move the folded section along the table so it hangs over the edge and paste the rest of the paper in the same way.

4 FOLDING THE PAPER
When you've finished pasting, fold the rest of the paper over, leaving a gap of about 2in (5cm) in the middle.

Some papers must be left for a few minutes for the paste to soak in or they will wrinkle when hung; follow the instructions on the roll label. Lay this paper to one side and paste the next length in the meantime.

5 LIFTING THE PAPER
When the paper is ready to be hung, drape it over your arm to carry it to the wall.

HANGING THE PAPER

1 HANGING THE FIRST LENGTH
Gently unfold the top of the paper. Slide it into position on the wall, with a trimming allowance of 2in (5cm) overlapping at the ceiling. Position one side edge of the paper along the pencil line. If it hangs off the line, don't try to force it into place; unpeel it carefully and start again.

2 BRUSHING ON THE PAPER
Using the paper-hanging brush, start in the center with vertical strokes, then brush sideways to push all the air bubbles out. Take plenty of time over this and don't stretch the paper. If the paper wrinkles, unpeel it and brush it back into place. Carefully unfold the lower part of the paper and brush it on in the same way.

HEAVYWEIGHT PAPERS

If you're hanging a heavyweight paper, coat the walls with size (a thinned mix of wallpaper paste) the day before. This seals the wall and allows you to adjust the paper much more easily. You should also apply size to old bare plaster, because it is very porous.

OBSTRUCTIONS

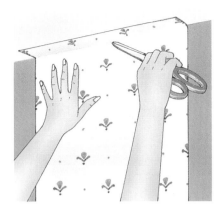

5 USING A SEAM ROLLER
To smooth the edges, go over the seams with a seam roller about 20 minutes after hanging. Do not roll embossed papers; dab seams firmly with the hanging brush instead.

3 TRIMMING THE PAPER
Use the end of the brush to push the surplus paper into the angle between the ceiling and the wall. Mark a cutting line by running the back of a scissor blade gently into the angle. Peel the paper back carefully and cut along the line. Brush the paper back and knock it in with the bristle tips. Trim against the baseboard in the same way. Wipe any paste off the ceiling and the baseboard with a damp sponge.

Mark paper to be trimmed against a window frame with scissors, then run a very sharp craft knife blade carefully down the mark to remove the surplus.

DOORS AND WINDOWS
If the paper overlaps the door or window frame by a large amount, cut it roughly to shape after pasting it, leaving 2in (5cm) at the top and side for trimming. (A large trim is heavy and liable to tear at the corner.) Brush the paper on at the top. Make a diagonal cut where it overlaps the corner of the frame until it can be eased into place. Knock it in with the bristle ends, mark the edge with the back of the scissors, and trim it, making horizontal cuts with scissors and vertical cuts with a craft knife.

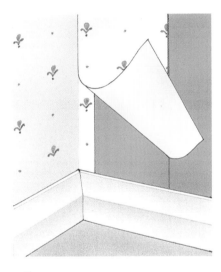

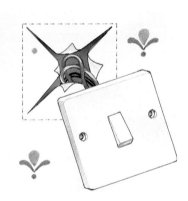

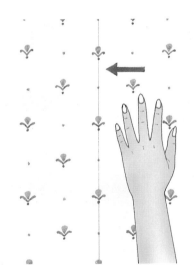

4 MATCHING THE PATTERN
Position the second length of paper so that the pattern lines up with the previous one, and push the paper up or down with your fingertips until the motifs align perfectly. Also push the paper sideways so that the two long edges are tightly butted together, with no overlaps or gaps anywhere.

6 TURNING CORNERS
When you reach a corner, do not try to turn a full width of paper onto the next wall – the angle between them is rarely square, so the paper will wrinkle. A length of paper that turns a corner should be hung as two strips.

Measure across the bare wall at the top and bottom. Trim a length of paper down to the widest measurement plus ¾in (20mm), so that the cut edge goes around the corner when hung. Hang this strip. Measure the width of the remaining paper and mark a vertical line on the second wall this distance away from the corner. Paste and hang the strip against the line, then brush it well down where it overlaps slightly. (If you are using vinyl, coat the lower piece with rubber-solution glue.)

Treat a chimney corner and other external corners in the same way, adding 1⅜in (3.5cm) to the widest measurement. Place the overlap on the side where it will be least conspicuous.

LIGHT SWITCHES AND SOCKET OUTLETS
Turn off the electricity. Loosen the screws so the fitting comes slightly away from the wall. Let the paper hang over it, then make diagonal cuts toward the corners with scissors. Slip the fitting through to the front, cut away the excess paper and brush the edges behind the fitting.

MARK THE SPOTS

Before papering, insert pieces of matchstick into any plugs in the walls where shelves or other fittings are to be replaced. Leave them sticking out just enough to feel through the paper.

WALLPAPER BORDERS

A dding a wallpaper border is a quick and easy way to introduce extra color or pattern to a room. It improves the proportions of an area visually and can link different patterns.

BORDER CHOICE

Wallpaper borders come in a wide choice of patterns and colors, and some are designed to coordinate with particular wallpapers. Some borders are self-adhesive, so you will not need to buy paste. Border widths range from about 1in (2.5cm) to 9½in (24cm), and rolls are usually 11yd (10m) long.

PLACING A BORDER

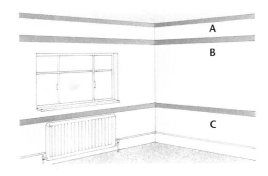

A: Just below ceiling level borders butt up to the ceiling, cornice, or coving for a neat finish.
B: Picture rail level borders help to reduce ceiling height visually. This effect is helped by painting the wall above the border in the same color as the ceiling. Picture rails are traditionally about 12-18in (30-45cm) below the ceiling.
C: Chair rail level borders can be used to coordinate different colors and patterns above and below the border. Chair rails are usually placed about 3ft (90cm) above the floor.

▲ *This border above painted paneled wood, at chair-rail height, coordinates with the curtains and wallpaper.*

SURFACES

Borders can be laid over most sound surfaces, including painted walls, woodwork, and wallpaper. They can also be laid over low-relief woodchip papers, although results are not always satisfactory, and they are unsuitable for heavily embossed wallpapers and textured plasters.

CALCULATING QUANTITIES

To work out how many rolls you need for your room, measure the length and width of the room, add the two together, and multiply by two. If the border is also going to run around a door or window, measure that area separately and add the figure to your total. Allow for error – if the total works out at exactly four rolls, buy five.

MATERIALS

Metal tape measure

Carpenter's level (optional)

Pencil

Long wooden batten

Special border paste

Paintbrush about the same width as your border

Worktable

Scissors

Wallpaper brush

Seam roller (optional)

Craft knife and ruler (optional)

Guidelines

You need a guideline to make sure that the border is hung straight; doing it by eye is not reliable. If you are laying a border against the ceiling or a picture or chair rail, use this as your guideline. Otherwise, follow the instructions below.

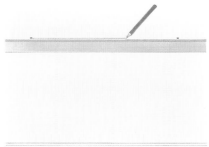

USING A CARPENTER'S LEVEL

Place your carpenter's level at the height you want the bottom of the border to rest. Make a horizontal pencil line at each end. Line up a long wooden batten with the pencil marks, then draw a line along its full length, joining the two marks.

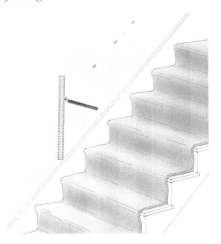

MEASURING METHOD

Use this method for drawing a guideline if you don't have a carpenter's level or if you are putting a border up a stairway. Mark the distance from the floor or ceiling at intervals along the wall. Line up a long wooden batten with the pencil marks, and join them with a faint pencil line.

EASY BORDERS

Self-adhesive borders are really easy to hang. Simply lay the strip gently in place, and when you are satisfied with the look, press it firmly against the wall. The border will then be stuck fast, and you will not be able to move it.

Hanging borders

Take your time when deciding how to place the patterns in the border at the corner of your room.

1 CUTTING THE FIRST PIECE
Using your original measurements, unroll a strip of border long enough to cover one wall. If the border is patterned, hold it against the wall to check the position of the pattern at each corner. Ideally, you should avoid cutting motifs. If you do have to cut a motif, decide where to cut for the best effect. Cut the strip, allowing an overlap of ½in (12mm) at each end.

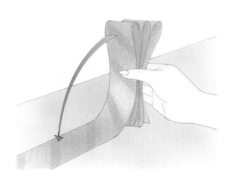

2 PASTING THE STRIP
Place the border face down on the worktable and apply a strip of paste down the center. Use a brush to spread the paste evenly over the whole border. Fold the border up accordion style so that you can hold it in one hand. Wipe the table before using it for the next strip.

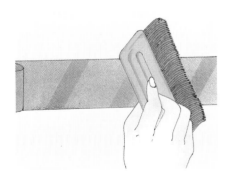

3 HANGING THE FIRST STRIP
Start in the right-hand corner if you are right-handed, and the left-hand corner if you are left-handed. Line up the border with the guideline. Unfold a workable length and lay it in position, pressing it down gently with the flat of your hand. Check the position, and when you are satisfied, smooth the border down firmly with a wallpaper brush, working from the center outward to expel air bubbles. Wipe off any excess paste.

4 HANGING THE SECOND STRIP
Take the border around the corner of the first wall. On the second wall, start with a slight overlap, adjusting and trimming to get the best pattern match. For best results, seal the join with a seam roller.

Mitering corners

Corners need special care when you are creating a panel or framing doors or windows. With some designs, you can cover the corner with a motif you have cut yourself, although you can buy special corner motifs for some borders. Plains, stripes, and some repeating patterns must be mitered at the corners for a really neat finished look.

1 PREPARING TO MITER
Cut and position the vertical strip, leaving a 6in (15cm) overlap beyond the top and bottom edges. Lay an unpasted horizontal strip in place. Don't cut the horizontal strip to length yet.

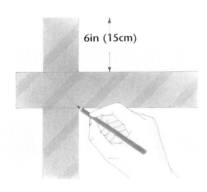

6in (15cm)

2 MARKING THE MITER
In pencil, mark on the vertical strip where the two strips intersect at the inner and outer points. On the horizontal strip, draw a straight line between these two marks. This line marks the angle of the miter. On the vertical section, cut along the line between the two pencil marks and then repaste the strip.

CORNER MOTIFS

Buy a special corner motif to create a neat finish on the corners of panels or to frame a door. If corner motifs are not available for the border you are using, you can cut out a motif from the border yourself and paste it in place.

3 MATCHING THE PATTERN
Lightly fold along the pencil line of the horizontal strip and place it against the vertical strip. Check the fit and the pattern match, adjusting the fold position if necessary. Make a sharp crease. If working around a door or window, lay both vertical strips first, then check the fit and pattern match at both corners before marking the horizontal piece with creases.

4 CUTTING THE CROSS STRIP
Cut along the crease using sharp scissors or a craft knife held against a ruler. Repeat with the opposite end, if you are mitering it also. Alternatively, trim it as required.

5 FINISHING THE CORNER
Paste the horizontal strip and butt it up to the vertical strip. Press it carefully but firmly into place and wipe off any excess paste. For really neat results, firm the join with a seam roller.

WALL-MOUNTED SHELVES

Every home has to have shelves, whether they're for storage or for displaying favorite ornaments or both. Putting up your own shelves is straightforward: you need very few skills, and shelving materials are widely available in home decorating stores and lumberyards.

SHELVING MATERIALS

There is a wide variety of both natural and human-made materials available for shelving. Many suppliers offer precut and finished shelving materials; others will cut shelves to size for you.

Blockboard. This is made from strips of softwood covered with wood veneer or melamine. It is quite rigid and good for medium to heavy loads. It can be varnished or primed and painted. Cut edges can be covered with wood veneer or plastic edging.

Chipboard. This comes in conveniently sized shelf widths, with either wood veneer or plastic coatings, and is inexpensive. It is not as strong as other shelving materials so it needs more support. You can cover cut edges with wood veneer or plastic edging.

Glass. This is a popular choice for display shelving. It is available from suppliers who will cut it to size and grind the edges smooth. Glass for shelving should be at least ¼in (6mm) thick.

Plywood. Made from thin layers of wood glued together horizontally, this is available with a wood veneer or plastic covering. Sold in sheets, it has to be cut to size. It is strong but not very rigid.

Fiberboard (Masonite™). This comes in sheets in a variety of thicknesses and has a smooth surface without a grain. As strong and stiff as chipboard, it can be varnished or primed and painted.

▼ Use this chart as a guide to the distance between supports for medium loads on solid walls. For heavy loads, such as books, put the brackets closer together.

Shelf kits. These come with precut and finished shelves made of wood or human-made boards, plus brackets and all the necessary fixings.

Wood. Wood is the strongest and least pliable shelving material and is excellent for carrying heavy loads. The most popular woods for shelving are softwoods, such as pine and redwood. Hardwoods, which include teak and mahogany, are much more expensive.

FIXINGS

Fix shelves to solid walls with screws and wall plugs. If you are fixing light shelves to hollow walls, use special anchor plugs; if the load is heavy, attach the fixings to the timber frame.

You must decide between 2in (50mm), 2¼in (60mm) or 3in (75mm) screws, depending on the size of shelf and the weight of the load it will carry. For light loads use a 6-gauge screw; for heavy loads, use a 10-gauge screw.

For shelving brackets, be sure to use short screws that won't break through the shelf.

SHELF SUPPORTS

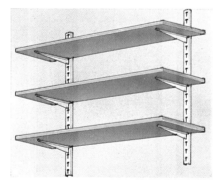

Adjustable track systems. With these you can change the spaces between the shelves. Wooden or metal uprights are fixed to the wall, then brackets, which hold the shelves, are slotted into them.

Angled metal strips. These support both the side edges of alcove shelving. They are unobtrusive and can support quite heavy loads.

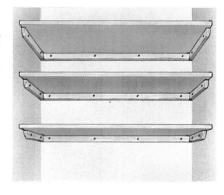

Battens. These are suitable for heavy shelving in alcoves. The battens are fixed to the three sides of the alcove, and the shelf is placed on top.

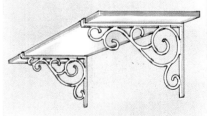

L-shaped brackets. These are fixed directly to the wall or to a batten. The shelf is usually screwed to the bracket, although the special brackets for glass shelves have a lip to secure the shelf. There is a wide range of brackets available in both metal and wood, some of them highly decorative.

MATERIAL	THICKNESS	DISTANCE
Blockboard	⅝ in (16mm)	23 ½ in (60cm)
Coated chipboard	⅝ in (16mm)	23 ½ in (60cm)
Masonite	⅝ in (16mm)	23 ½ in (60cm)
Plywood	⅝ in (16mm)	23 ½ in (60cm)
Blockboard	¾ in (19mm)	27 ½ in (70cm)
Chipboard	¾ in (19mm)	27 ½ in (70cm)
Masonite	¾ in (19mm)	27 ½ in (70cm)
Wood	¾ in (19mm)	27 ½ in (70cm)
Glass	⅜ in (10mm)	27 ½ in (70cm)

Cord supports. These look stylish but are unsuitable for heavy loads. The cords are fixed to screws on the wall and are then threaded through the shelves. The cords can either be knotted underneath each shelf or secured to screws on the wall beneath the shelf.

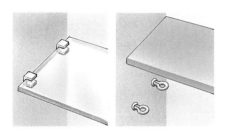

Studs. These are used for lightweight shelving in alcoves. They are unobtrusive and come in a range of styles. They are fixed to the wall at the sides of the alcove: the shelf can rest on top or slot into them, depending on the type of shelf or stud.

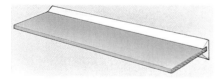

Slotted supports. These are specially shaped strips that are fixed to the wall. The shelf slots into a channel in the strip. These supports are unobtrusive and come in a range of colors and lengths, which you can cut to size.

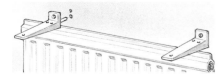

Cantilever brackets. These are unobtrusive plastic brackets that can only be used on solid walls. They're ideal for securing shelves where there isn't enough room for a standard bracket; for example, over a radiator.

Securing a fixed-bracket shelf

Fixed-bracket shelves are supported by wall brackets. The method shown below is suitable for small shelves. Ask a friend to hold the shelf horizontal while you fix it in position. If you are fixing a heavy or large shelf, see LARGE OR HEAVY SHELVES (below).

MATERIALS

Shelving, cut to size

Brackets

Pencil

Carpenter's level

Metal tape

Screws

Bradawl (for softwood and human-made boards) or twist bit (for hardwood)

Screwdriver

Drill and masonry bit

Screws and plugs for solid walls or hollow walls

1 POSITIONING THE SHELF
Hold the shelf against the wall in the required position. With a pencil, mark its top edge. Remove the shelf. Using a carpenter's level, draw a horizontal line on the wall at the shelf position.

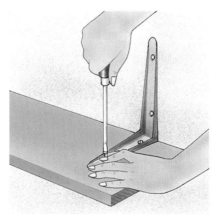

2 ATTACHING THE BRACKETS
Decide how far apart to place the brackets, using the table opposite as a guide. Lay the shelf with the underside facing upwards. Place one bracket in position with the longer arm flush with the back edge of the shelf. Mark the screw holes with a pencil and screw the bracket to the shelf. Fix the other bracket(s) in the same way.

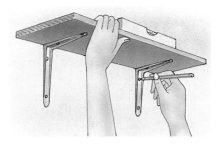

3 MARKING THE HOLES
Align the shelf with the pencil line on the wall. Use the carpenter's level to check that it is horizontal. Mark the positions for the fixings through the fixing holes in the brackets. Drill the wall at the marks and insert the plugs.

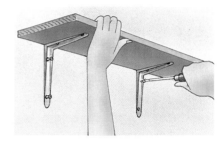

4 ATTACHING THE SHELF
Holding the shelf in position, drive in one fixing screw per bracket, tightening each screw halfway only. Then drive in the remaining fixing screws and tighten them all up.

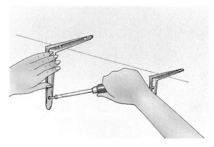

LARGE OR HEAVY SHELVES
If you are fixing a large or heavy shelf, it is easier to fix the brackets to the wall first. Then position the shelf on the brackets, and screw the brackets to the shelf.

ATTACHING SEVERAL SHELVES
Secure the top shelf first, then hang a plumb line over one short end. Line up the shelves below with the string. Alternatively, hang the plumb line from one of the brackets, and line up the brackets on the shelves below with the string.

CHAIR RAILS

Lengths of wooden molding fixed around a room at waist height are known as chair rails. The Victorians used them to stop chair backs marking the wall, but nowadays they are used to improve the proportions of a room and to add decorative impact. They are a very effective way of dividing different wall treatments: for instance, you could have a durable wallpaper below the chair rail and a more fragile paint effect above it.

DECORATING CHAIR RAILS

Chair rails can be primed and painted, varnished, stained, or color-rubbed in exactly the same way as any other internal woodwork.

It is easier to sand the rail so that it's ready for decorating before you cut it and fix it in place. Paint or varnish the wood after you have fixed it in position, and use masking tape to protect the walls. For information on preparing wood for decorating, refer to pages 140–41.

BUYING CHAIR RAIL MOLDING

You can buy chair rails from lumberyards. Traditional chair rail is 1½-3in (4-7.5cm) wide and 1in (2.5cm) deep. It has decorative molding along the front, with a flat section down the center. You can also use narrower picture-rail molding.

If you're a beginner, it's best to start off with plain, narrow molding made of softwood. You'll find that softwood moldings are easier to saw through than hardwood ones and also they are less expensive.

To calculate how much molding you need, measure the walls and add 2¼yd (2m) for wastage.

MATERIALS

Chair rail molding

Metal tape and pencil

Long carpenter's level

Tenon saw and miter box

Brads and hammer

Panel or construction adhesive

Fine sandpaper

Plastic wood and cellulose filler

Primer and paint or clear polyurethane varnish

PREPARATION WORK

1 MARKING THE GUIDELINE
Mark the height of the lower edge of the chair rail at intervals on the wall – the usual height is about 3ft (90cm) from the floor. Line up the marks with a long carpenter's level, then draw a pencil line along its length, joining the marks. Continue working around the room in the same way. Your starting and finishing points must align.

2 PLANNING THE LAYOUT
To check that the joins will not fall at awkward places, lay the molding on the floor next to the walls and work out where to make any cuts and joins. Start at a door frame or window. Where possible, avoid placing joins just before corners, as this makes cutting difficult, or on narrow stretches of wall, where one piece of molding could go right across.

USING A MITER BOX

The only really accurate way of cutting wood at 45° angles (miters) is to use a miter box with a tenon saw. A combination square or set square allows you to mark the angles but does not guide the saw during cutting. Miter boxes also have a straight slot for cutting wood at 90° (right angles). Do a few practice cuts on scrap timber to get the idea before you start cutting a molding.

Saw very carefully when you get close to the bottom of the molding to prevent the wood from splitting.

1 PREPARING THE MITER BOX
Use a bench hook to hold the miter box steady, or screw it to a work bench. Lay a scrap piece of wood in the bottom of the box to protect it from saw damage and to ensure a clean cut.

2 CUTTING THE MITER
Put the molding in the box and slip the tenon saw into one pair of the angled slots in the box, making sure that the cut slopes the required way. Holding the molding firmly and the saw horizontally, cut through the molding until you reach the scrap wood underneath.

◄ Position your chair rail about 3ft (90cm) above the floor, or level with the bottom of the window.

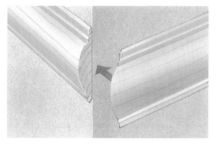

CUTTING THE WOOD

At corners and joins, always make miter cuts. Use the miter box, as described in USING A MITER BOX on the previous page. Make a straight (90°) cut at windows and doors using the miter box.

CUTTING THE FIRST LENGTH

Measure the length of the first wall you are going to fit with the chair rail. You will need a length of molding at least 2in (5cm) longer than this.

When you have made your first cut, measure and mark the length required on the *back* of the molding, then make the second mitered cut.

CUTTING EXTERNAL CORNERS

Position a length of molding in the miter box, lining it up at least 1in (2.5cm) beyond the angled slots. Put the tenon saw in the slots so that the cut face of the molding will slope toward the flat side of the timber. Cut the wood.

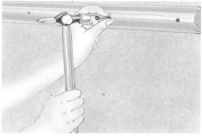

CUTTING INTERNAL CORNERS

Put the molding in the miter box and hold it upright against the back wall. Position the end to be trimmed about 1in (2.5cm) beyond one of the diagonal slots in the box, so that the cut face will slope to the molded side of the timber. Cut the molding with the tenon saw. Measure and mark the length required on the back of the molding before making the second miter or straight cut.

JOINING LENGTHS OF MOLDING

If you need more than one length of molding to span the wall, cut and fit one piece at a time, starting in a corner. Make miter cuts. Sand the cut edges lightly before fixing together.

GLUING ON A CHAIR RAIL

Ask a friend to come and help when you are ready to fix the chair rail in place. The easiest method of fixing the rail to the wall is to use panel or construction adhesive (see below). However, you can use masonry nails if you prefer (see right).

1 PREPARING THE WALL
Mark a guideline on the wall and plan the layout of the molding (see PREPARATION WORK, on the previous page). Cut the molding to length, as shown above, mitering it at joins and corners. Use the hammer to knock a row of brads into the walls along the guideline; but don't hammer the brads all the way in.

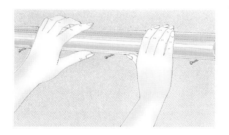

2 ATTACHING THE CHAIR RAIL
Spread the adhesive along the back of the molding. Press it in position with the lower edge resting on the brads. Let the glue set, then remove the brads.

3 FINISHING
Fill any gaps with cellulose filler, or use plastic wood if you want a clear finish. Sand the filler when it's dry, then decorate the chair rail with paint or stain and varnish.

NAILING ON A CHAIR RAIL

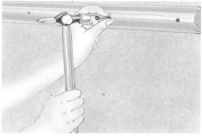

Using a wood bit, drill pilot holes in the rail for the masonry nails. Put one near each end and others about 18in (45cm) apart. Hold the chair molding against the wall, over the guideline, and drive in a nail at each end, then add the remaining nails. Use a nail punch to hammer the nail heads below the surface and fill in the holes with plastic wood. To finish, see step 3, left.

REDECORATING INTERIOR DOORS

It does not take much expertise to improve the look of an interior door. For example, you could add beading (narrow, shaped strips of wood) to a flat door to imitate the look of paneling or replace the door handles or add a fingerplate to complement a new color scheme.

Applying beading

Follow the steps below to give a flush (flat-fronted) door a paneled look with lengths of beading. It's simple to do, as long as you miter the end of each length to make neat corners.

When you're planning the panels, make sure the arrangement is symmetrical across the whole width of the door. Place the panels 4in (10cm) from the side edges. The horizontal gaps between the panels can be up to 8in (20cm) wide.

Either paint or stain and varnish the beading to match the door surface, or decorate it in a different color so that it stands out.

MATERIALS

Beading

Miter box

Tenon saw

Brads

Small hammer

Sandpaper

Long metal ruler

T-square

Pencil

Masking tape

Brown paper

Wood filler

Paint or varnish

PANELING KITS

It's easy to panel a door if you use a panel kit that contains ready-mitered beading. Beading and paneling kits are both available in different sizes and finishes from most large home decorating stores.

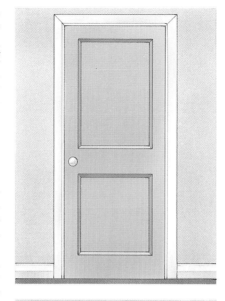

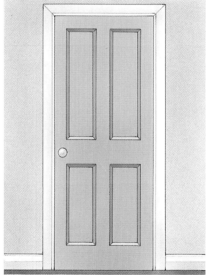

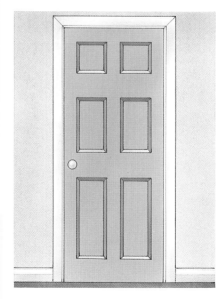

1 PLANNING THE PANELS
Decide if you want two, four, or six panels. Draw them on brown paper, cut them out, and tape them to the door.

2 MARKING THE DOOR
Using the long ruler, T-square, and pencil, mark the outline of each panel on the front of the door to help you position the beading.

3 MITERING THE BEADING
Measure the width and height of each panel, and note how many pieces of beading of each size you will need. Mark the required length on the beading, measuring from the outer edge of the first miter and cutting the second miter in the reverse direction. Measure and cut additional sections of beading, mitering the ends to make neat corners. Sand the cut ends lightly to remove any rough areas, but take care not to round off the miters.

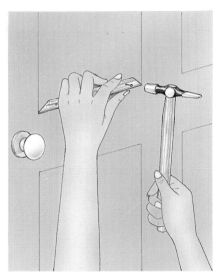

4 NAILING ON THE BEADING
Partially drive in a brad near each end of the first length of beading. Then place the beading on the door, aligning it with the pencil marks, and tap in the brads. If necessary, space additional brads in-between.

5 COMPLETING A PANEL
Repeat with the other three lengths to complete the first panel, aligning the miters carefully and checking that the corners are square.

6 FINISHING
Complete the other panels in the same way, checking that the verticals and horizontals are aligned across the door. Punch in the brads and fill in any holes or cracks in the mitered joins with the wood filler. Paint or varnish the door and the beading.

Replacing a handle

Whatever the style of the handle or doorknob you choose, the fitting procedure is much the same, but you should follow the manufacturer's instructions for the size and positioning of the fixing holes.

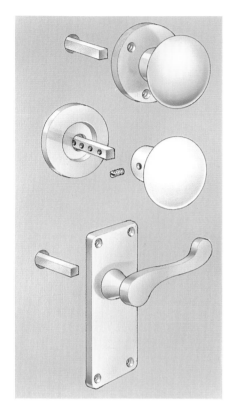

Two types of doorknob are commonly used on interior doors: screw-on and door-mounted. The screw-on version has a small grub screw at the base of the knob that secures it to the spindle running through the door. This is the more attractive, since the fixing is not visible. The door-mounted type has a plate with the knob attached, and the plate screws directly into the door. Handles are usually door-mounted.

MATERIALS
New doorknob or handle
Screws
Screwdriver
Wood filler
Wood stain (for varnished doors)
Varnish (for varnished doors)
Sandpaper
Filling knife

1 REMOVING THE OLD HANDLE
Using a screwdriver, undo the screws holding the old door handle in position. Slide the handle off the spindle.

2 FILLING IN THE OLD HOLES
With the filling knife and a small amount of filler, plug any screw holes that will show when the new doorknob or handle is fitted. On a varnished wooden door, tint the filler with stain to match the color of the wood. When the filler is dry, sand it down until smooth. Touch up the filled area with varnish.

3 FITTING THE NEW DOORKNOB
Place the new knob or handle on the spindle. If the doorknob screws onto the spindle, make sure that the screw hole is on the underside. Attach the knob or handle according to the screw fitting.

Adding a fingerplate

Some doorknobs are available with matching fingerplates, or you can buy a plain fingerplate to coordinate with the existing handle or knob.

MATERIALS
Fingerplate
Ruler
Carpenter's level
Pencil
Screws
Bradawl
Screwdriver or drill

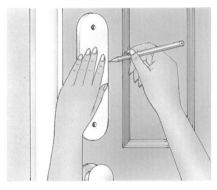

1 POSITIONING THE FINGERPLATE
Position the fingerplate roughly 2in (5cm) above the doorknob. Using a ruler and carpenter's level, make sure that it is parallel to the edge of the door. Using the pencil, mark the position of the edges and the screws.

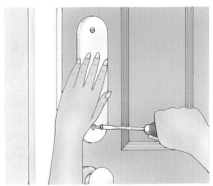

2 FITTING THE FINGERPLATE
Start the screw holes with a bradawl or fine drill hole. Secure the plate to the door with screws.

PREPARING CURTAINS

Curtains require only basic sewing skills; even beginners can achieve good results. The key to success is accurate measuring and careful cutting. Use a metal ruler or metal tape measure, take your time, and double check your work.

Before you do anything, decide on the finished length of the curtains and the style of heading. Always measure the window with the track or pole in position, and check the width at both the top and bottom of the window in case it is not quite square. If you are making curtains for more than one window, measure each separately, even if they look the same.

Lined curtains will need the same amount of lining fabric as main fabric. Lining-fabric widths are cut and joined in exactly the same way as described for the main-fabric widths.

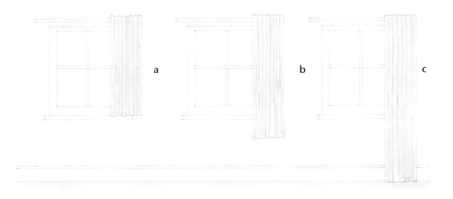

MATERIALS

Metal ruler or metal tape measure

Pencil and paper

Calculator (optional)

Tailor's chalk

Pins

Scissors

Large, flat surface

LENGTH

There are three standard lengths for curtains: sill length (**a**), just below the sill (**b**), and floor length (**c**).

Sill-length curtains usually fall about ⅜in (10mm) above the sill so that they sweep just clear of it.

Curtains **just below sill length** look best if they hang 4-6in (10-15cm) below the sill.

Floor-length curtains should normally hang ⅜in (10mm) above the floor to prevent wear and soilage. If you want the curtains to bunch onto the floor, however, add another 2-8in (5-20cm) to the finished length. Curtains that fall between any of these standard lengths will tend to look unbalanced.

WIDTH

The type of heading you want for your curtains will determine the width of fabric needed. You will need to multiply the finished width of the curtain *at least* 1½-2 times to achieve the necessary fullness: with sheers and other very lightweight fabrics multiply by 3.

SHRINKAGE

Watch out for fabrics that may shrink when they are first washed. If you have chosen washable fabric for your curtains and think that it may shrink, buy an extra 4in (10cm) per yard (meter). Then either wash the fabric to shrink it before cutting it out, or make up the curtains with the extra fabric turned up in the bottom hem. You can then adjust the length after the first wash.

Measuring

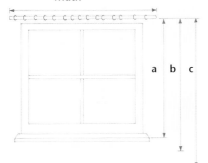

width

a b c

1 MEASURING THE LENGTH

For the fabric length, measure the finished length of the curtain (a, b, or c) from the top of the track or from the bottom of the curtain pole. If the curtain heading will project above the track, or hang below it, adjust the measurement accordingly.

2 ADDING ALLOWANCES

Add an allowance of about 1½in (4cm) for the heading and 6in (15cm) for the hem to give the total cut fabric length for each curtain. Double the hem allowance for sheer fabrics.

3 FINDING THE WIDTH

For the fabric width, measure the pole or track. Multiply this figure by the amount required to give the necessary fullness (see above). Then add on 1in (2.5cm) for each side hem allowance, or 2in (5cm) for sheers. This gives you the **total curtain width**. Note: if you need more than one fabric width per curtain, because the total curtain width is greater than the fabric width, add on seam allowances as well.

CALCULATING FABRIC QUANTITIES

First calculate the number of fabric widths needed to cover the window: simply divide the **total curtain width** by the width of your chosen fabric. Round up this figure to the next full number if necessary. For example, if you work out that you will need 4.6 widths to cover a window, you will have to round up this figure to allow for 5 widths.

To calculate the total fabric quantity needed, multiply the number of fabric widths by the **cut fabric length**. This quantity of fabric is then divided between the number of curtains that are required.

If the fabric has a prominent design, allow for one extra fabric repeat per fabric width.

CUTTING

When you are cutting, work on a large, flat surface such as a big table or the floor. Remember that the curtains will hang well only if you start with a straight cut across the width.

1 POSITIONING THE PATTERN
Lay the fabric flat and check the direction of the pattern, if any. Position large motifs at the hem edge of the curtain, so that any half motifs will be disguised by the heading.

2 STRAIGHTENING THE FABRIC END
Make sure the end of the fabric is perfectly straight. To do this, pull out a thread across the width to make a guide for your cutting line. Alternatively, cut at a right angle to the selvages using a ruler.

3 CUTTING THE FABRIC
Measure and cut the first length. To cut the next piece, place the first cut length against the uncut fabric and match the design across. Then cut out the next length so that it finishes and ends at exactly the same point of the pattern as the first piece. Continue like this until you have cut all the widths you need.

JOINING PATTERNED FABRIC WIDTHS

1 MATCHING THE PATTERN
Lay one curtain width on a flat surface. Turn under the seam allowance on the second width and, with the pattern matching exactly, place it over the seam allowance of the first width. Pin at right angles to the join.

2 JOINING THE WIDTHS
Tack firmly down the join. Then, machine-stitch the seam in the normal way. If you are joining selvages, use a flat seam. For frayed edges and sheer curtains, use a French or a fell seam.

French and fell seams

French and fell seams are both enclosed seams, which means that the raw edges are enclosed within the seam. Because of this, these seams are both neat and strong, making them ideal for sheer fabrics, such as net curtains, as well as garments that will take heavy wear, such as children's clothes.

Both fell and French seams fall on the reverse of the fabric. With fell seams, one stitching line is visible on the right side, but with French seams, no stitching line is visible. Fell seams should not be confused with flat fell seams, which fall on the right side of the fabric.

FRENCH SEAM

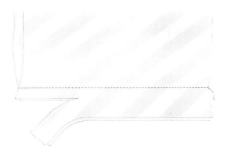

1 STITCHING THE WRONG SIDES
With *wrong sides* together, stitch a ⅜ in (10mm) seam. Trim the seam to ⅛ in (3mm), then press it.

2 COMPLETING THE SEAM
Fold the right sides together so that the seamline is exactly on the fold. Press. Stitch ¼ in (6mm) from fold. Press the seam to one side.

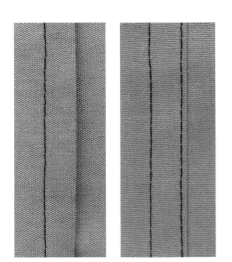

FELL SEAM

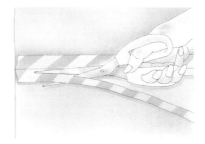

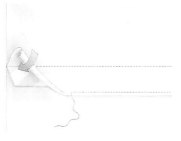

1 STITCHING THE SEAM
With right sides together, stitch a ⅝ in (15mm) seam. Press open and trim off half of one seam allowance.

2 ENCLOSING THE ALLOWANCES
Fold the other seam allowance over the trimmed one, as shown above, and tack it down so that the raw edge is enclosed. Stitch through all the layers.

Blinds

Especially if space is limited or if a window is awkwardly placed, blinds are an attractive alternative to curtains. They can also be used with curtains to provide additional shade or privacy.

The main types of fabric blinds are listed below, together with diagrams showing their front and back views so that you can see what they look like and how they are constructed. The roller blind looks the same on both sides. The blinds pictured are alternatives to the well-known and commonly used Venetian blinds.

ROLLER BLINDS

A roller blind is a very economical window covering. It is a flat blind that rolls around a piece of wooden dowel (called the roller), fitted with a spring mechanism. The bottom edge of the blind is held straight by a strip of wood inserted in a casing. The blind is raised and lowered by pulling a cord on the bottom edge.

Roller blinds are made from unlined, stiffened fabric. You can buy fabric ready-stiffened or stiffen your own with a liquid or spray stiffener. The bottom and side edges of the blind can be shaped into decorative scallops, and the lower edge is sometimes decorated with trims such as braid or lace.

AUSTRIAN BLINDS

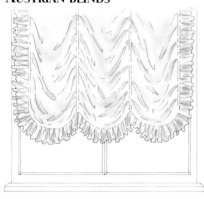
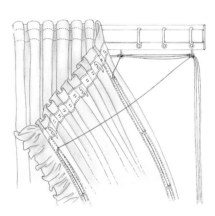

Austrian blinds (flounced blinds) are gathered vertically into flounced panels when they are raised, and when lowered, the bottom gathers into a few soft folds. They can be made from curtain-weight fabrics or sheers.

The blinds are gathered horizontally with curtain heading tape and they are raised by a series of cords threaded through rings on the back. They can be hung from standard tracks attached to a batten.

FESTOON BLINDS

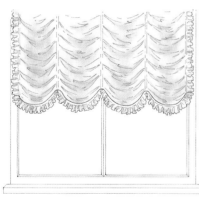
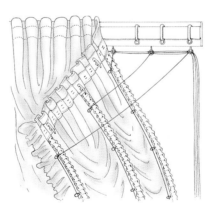

Festoon blinds resemble Austrian blinds when they are raised, but the flounces are permanent: when the blind is lowered, it keeps its gathered appearance. Special festoon tape is used to gather the blinds vertically into flounces. Festoon blinds are often made from unlined sheer fabric, and are used either on their own or teamed with sheer curtains. They often have frills around the edges, which enhances the frilly effect.

ROMAN BLINDS

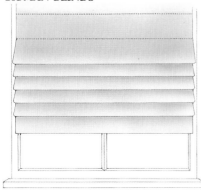

Roman blinds lie flat against the window, but they fold into neat horizontal pleats when they are pulled up. They are often fitted with horizontal slats of wood, which give definition to the pleats, but for a softer effect the blinds can be made without these. Cords, threaded through rings attached to the slats or at regular intervals, raise and lower the blind.

Roman blinds are often lined and can be made from most furnishing fabrics but not flimsy, sheer fabrics.

TRACKS AND TAPES FOR BLINDS

Specialty tracks and tapes for blinds are available in an enormous range, so here is a guide to help you pick out the items you require. If you don't want to use specialized equipment, you can adapt standard tracks or tapes.

Tracks

Net rods. Lightweight, permanently lowered blinds can be threaded onto slim net rods or covered curtain wire.

Standard track. You can hang your blind from a standard curtain track, but you'll need to fix the track onto a wooden batten and insert screw eyes into this to thread the cords through. Nail the batten straight onto the wall or secure it with angle brackets. If the track is already in place, fix the screw eyes into the window frame or into a wooden batten fixed below the track.

Track for festoon blinds. Use this to hang Roman and Austrian blinds as well. It has cord holders on the lower edge to hold the cords that raise and lower the blind. The blind is attached to the track with standard curtain hooks. These tracks are flexible enough to bend around bay windows.

Wooden batten. You can hang a Roman blind from a wooden batten. Staple it to the batten, or hang it from touch-and-close tape (Velcro). Fix the batten in place with angle brackets. You can also use wooden battens to modify standard tracks for other blinds.

Tapes

Austrian blind tape. This translucent tape holds the cords that raise the blind. It's ¾in (20mm) wide and has fine loops to hold the cords.

Festoon blind tape. This translucent tape has thread loops or tiny plastic rings down one edge through which the cords that raise the blind are threaded. The tape pulls up the blind into soft, permanent folds.

Grip tape. This is used for hanging lightweight blinds and curtains. It consists of a pencil-pleat heading grip tape that grips another self-adhesive tape. The second tape is stuck to the top of the window. The two tapes are sold separately.

Pencil-pleat tape. This is suitable for gathering the top of Austrian and festoon blinds. On sheer fabrics use a translucent tape. You can also use standard heading tape.

Standard tape. This tape can be used instead of Austrian blind tape to gather up the fabric vertically. You'll need to sew small plastic rings along one edge to carry the cords.

Velcro fastening. This can be used to hang Roman blinds on wooden battens. One-half of the tape is stuck onto the front of the batten and the other half is sewn onto the top of the blind. The blind is then simply pressed in place onto the batten.

Kits

You can buy kits to make Austrian, Roman, and festoon blinds. They come in two sizes: for windows up to 48in (122cm) wide and for those up to 72in (183cm) wide. The kits contain everything you need except the track and the fabric.

Roller-blind kits include a wooden roller with a spring mechanism that you will have to cut to fit the window, a wooden slat for the bottom casing, two holding brackets, a pin end and a cap to fit over the free end of the roller, a cord holder, and acorn.

Useful fittings

Acorns. These are used to neaten the knotted ends of the pulley cords. They are generally made of wood, plastic, or china. You can buy novelty designs shaped like animals or flowers.

Cleats. Secure the blind cords to a cleat to keep the blind raised. Cleats come in a range of sizes and can be made of metal, coated metal, or brass.

Cord tidy. This holds the heading tape cords together and out of the way. It is slotted into the heading tape.

Screw eyes. These fittings are used with blinds mounted on wooden battens and standard track. They are fixed to the underside of the batten and the cords are threaded through them.

track for festoon blinds

acorn

covered curtain wire

slat

roller

cord tidy

screw eyes

cleat

grip tape

plastic rings

Austrian blind tape

standard tape

pencil-pleat heading grip tape

festoon blind tape

translucent pencil-pleat tape

Velcro tape

DECORATIVE BOWS

Bows make terrific trimmings for accessories and soft furnishings. Use them to give new life to dresses and bags, curtains, valances, tablecloths, and cushions. You can also use them to coordinate items: if you're making contrasting tiebacks for your curtains, add a bow in the curtain fabric so they match.

Here are just some of the bows you can make. Seam allowances of ⅝in (15mm) are included throughout.

One-piece bow

This is the easiest bow to make. It's ideal for making a quick curtain tieback, for securing a cushion to an upright chair, and for an instant decoration on clothing. Bows made in this way have a relaxed style that suits all but the most formal settings. They can have straight, slanting, or V-shaped tails.

1 CUTTING OUT THE FABRIC
Decide on the bow width and double the measurement, adding 1¼in (3cm) for seam allowances. To calculate the length, tie a tape measure into a bow of the required size, note the length and add 1¼in (3cm) for seam allowances. Cut out a strip of fabric to these measurements.

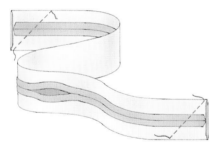

2 STITCHING THE BOW
Fold the fabric in half lengthwise with right sides together. Pin and stitch the long seam, leaving a gap in the center to turn through. Press the seam open and center it. Stitch across the ends, either straight or at an angle. Trim the seam allowances across the corners and turn the tube right side out through the gap in the seam. Slipstitch the gap closed and press the fabric.

3 TYING THE BOW
Tie a knot in the center of the fabric, then thread one end through the knot. Thread the other end through the knot, and pull the loops to make a neat bow.

QUICK RIBBON BOW
Use this method to tie an even ribbon, tape, or braid bow.

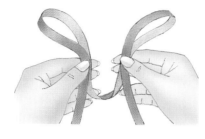

MAKING THE LOOPS
Cut a length of ribbon, tape, or braid and fold it in half to find the center. Form two equal loops about ½in (12mm) on each side of the center, as shown.

TYING THE BOW
Cross the loop in your left hand over the loop in your right hand, tuck it over the loop in your right hand and through the center gap. Pull the loops tight and adjust them.

Picture bow

Picture bows look best if they are made from crisp fabrics that hold their shape well. However, if you are using a fine fabric, interface it first to give it more body.

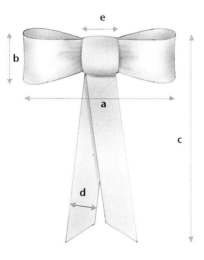

1 CUTTING OUT
For the loops, cut a fabric strip twice the width of the bow (**a**) plus ⅝in (15mm) by twice the depth of the loops (**b**) plus 1¼in (3cm). For the tails, cut a piece twice the length of each tail (**c**) plus 1¼in (3cm) by twice the width (**d**) plus 1¼in (3cm). For the knot, cut a piece twice the width of the knot (**e**) plus 1¼in (3cm) by 4¾in (12cm).

2 STITCHING THE LOOPS
Fold the loop strip in half lengthwise with right sides facing. Stitch the long edges; press the seam. Turn it out and center the seam. Zigzag across the ends. Gather into a bow as for BOW WITH A CONTRAST LINING, step 2 (opposite).

3 STITCHING THE TAILS
Fold the tail fabric in half with right sides facing and pin it. Stitch both long edges and across the ends, either straight or at an angle, leaving a gap in one long edge to turn through. Trim the seam allowances at the corners and turn the fabric out. Press it, then slipstitch the gap closed.

4 ASSEMBLING THE BOW
Make the knot as for BOW WITH A CONTRAST LINING, step 4 (opposite). Wrap it around the loop piece and stitch it to the back, trimming it if necessary. Fold the tails in half and stitch the fold to the back of the bow. Stitch a small curtain ring to the back of the knot and use this to hang the bow from a picture hook just above your picture.

Bow with a contrast lining

These bows take a bit longer to make than one-piece bows, but they are well worth the effort. They have a chic look that is perfect for sophisticated clothes and soft furnishings. Use them to make shoe bows, stitch them down the front of a jacket, or add them to the top of a formal curtain heading. You can make them with or without tails.

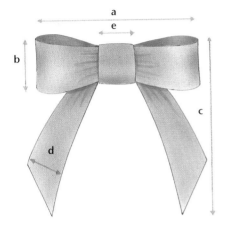

1 CUTTING THE FABRIC
Decide on the size of your bow. For the loops, cut one piece of main fabric twice the width of the bow (**a**) plus 1¼in (3cm) by the depth of the loops (**b**) plus 1¼in (3cm). For the tails (optional), cut one piece twice the length of the tail (**c**) plus ⅝in (15mm) by the depth of the tail (**d**) plus 1¼in (3cm). Cut these pieces from lining too. For the knot, cut a rectangle of main fabric twice the width of the finished knot (**e**) plus 1¼in (3cm) by 4¾in (12cm).

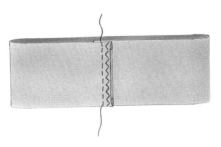

2 MAKING THE LOOPS
Pin the lining and main loop pieces together with right sides facing. Stitch both long seams. Turn the fabric tube right side out and press it. Zigzag across the ends to neaten them. Lay out the strip, lining side up, and bring the ends to the center, overlapping them by ⅝in (15mm). Using matching thread, stitch across the center through all layers and gather up the fabric slightly.

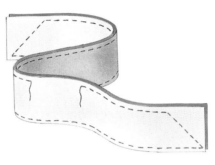

3 MAKING THE TAILS
Pin the lining and main tail pieces right sides together. Stitch them down one long edge and across both ends, either straight or at an angle. Stitch the remaining long edge, leaving a gap in the center. Trim the seams at the corners and turn the tails out. Press the tails, then slipstitch the gap closed.

4 MAKING THE KNOT
Fold the knot fabric in half lengthwise with right sides together and stitch the long seam. Center the seam and press it open. Turn the fabric out and zigzag-stitch each end.

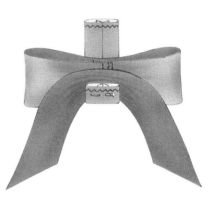

5 ATTACHING THE KNOT
Place the bow loops centrally over the tails. Fold the knot over the center of the bow loops and pin the ends at the back, behind the tails. Trim the knot piece if necessary. Using matching thread, slipstitch the ends together and to the back of the bow.

Wired sheer bow

Lace and sheer bows have a lovely, delicate quality that suits very feminine settings. These bows also look super on hats. They are made from strips of lace or sheer ribbon, kept in shape by fine florist's wire. Make the bows with double loops, with smaller loops on top. You can stitch on beads, sequins, or pearls for added glamour. For speed, you could use wired ribbon.

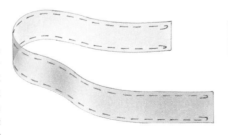

1 MAKING THE LOOPS
Cut a length of insertion lace or wide, sheer ribbon twice the width of the bow plus ⅝in (15mm). Cut a slightly shorter length for the top loops. Cut two pieces of wire the same length as each lace or ribbon strip. Weave the wire in and out of the lace or ribbon along each side edge. Bend the ends of the wire back on themselves to hold the wire in place.

2 ASSEMBLING THE BOW
Turn under the ends of each strip. Bend it into a ring and sew the ends together. Center the seam and press each ring into shape. Place the smaller loop on top of the larger one and stitch them together at the center. Cover the center with a strip of lace or ribbon as for BOW WITH A CONTRAST LINING, step 5 (above).

beaded stems

MOTIFS AND TRIMS

Accessory departments and fabric stores are full of ready-made motifs and other trims, that can be sewn, glued, or ironed onto soft furnishings, such as pillows and cushions.

When choosing a trim, check that the cleaning instructions are compatible with the article to be trimmed and follow any specific application instructions carefully, paying special attention to delicate fabrics.

Here is a list of some of the most popular and widely available motifs and trims.

Beaded motifs are usually made from fabric or lace and decorated with beads. They can be entirely covered with beads so that no fabric shows, or they may have just a few beads sewn around the edge or in the center. They can be made with glass, fake jet, pearl, or crystal beads, and can be used on lampshades and tableclothes. Modern motifs made with unusual beads, such as wood and fake coral, are also available. Sew-on beaded motifs should be pinned or tacked in position, then oversewn in place all around the edge of the motif, stitching between the beads. Iron-on beaded motifs have a fusible backing and are even easier to attach. They usually have a backing paper that is removed to reveal a slightly tacky surface. Press the motif into position on the right side of the fabric, then turn it to the wrong side, cover it with a clean cloth, and press it firmly with an iron heated to the appropriate setting.

Beaded stems are made from bunches of nylon strands, threaded with tiny pearls or beads, and bound together to form a spray. Hand-sew them in position with tiny stitches around each individual stem at either side of the binding.

Cord rosettes, tufts, and knots are traditional soft furnishing trimmings that are still popular. Ornate cord rosettes are expensive but give a sophisticated finish to draperies or bolsters. Woolen or linen tufts may be used in place of buttons on deep-buttoned chairs and sofas, or scattered on cushions, valances, and various other items. Intricate knots of cord that make a perfectly round ball are known as Turks head knots. They may be used as tiny buttons or as a decorative trim.

Crystals and fake jewels are available with holes, for sewing in place, and without holes, for gluing in place; special glues are available for this purpose. Some jewels have a claw setting incorporating needle tunnels for easy attachment. The jewels may be plain or faceted and are usually foiled at the back.

Embroidered motifs may be solidly embroidered or delicately embroidered onto organza and trimmed with pearls. Sew or iron them in place in the same way as the fabric motifs.

Fabric flowers are available in a great variety of sizes, colors, and species. Silk flowers have a slight sheen and lustrous coloring. Cotton flowers tend to be bolder and simpler. Velvet flowers have a heavier, baroque quality and come in rich, deep colors.

Fabric motifs are ready-made appliqués, made from one, two, or more contrasting fabrics. The edges are neatened with satin stitch and they sometimes have embroidered details or are lightly quilted. There are two types of appliqué motifs: sew-on motifs and iron-on motifs. Pin and tack sew-on motifs in position, then oversew them in place around the edges, taking small, closely spaced stitches in matching thread and following the direction of the satin stitches. For iron-on motifs, check the manufacturer's instructions. In general, position the motif, lay a clean,

beaded motif

woolen tuft

cord rosette

embroidered motifs

fake jewels

fabric flower

fabric motif

lace motif

large ribbon rose

thread-covered ball

tassels

damp cloth over the top, and press firmly with a medium iron for 20-30 seconds.

Feathers are available in their natural form or in a dazzling array of colors. The method of attachment depends on the article and type of fabric being trimmed. On a hat, for example, the base of the quill may be glued in place and covered with a bow or a flower, or sewn in place with matching thread.

Lace motifs are made from delicate, filigree lace suitable for trimming fine silk or cotton lawn; medium-weight cotton lace, useful for cushions and pillowcases; and heavy guipure lace, often used on bridal and evening wear. White and cream lace motifs may be trimmed with fake pearls or crystals. Other popular colors are ecru, mocha, and black.

The motifs can be oversewn in place by hand, with small, closely spaced stitches all around the edge, or machine-stitched just inside the edge, using a small, close zigzag stitch. If desired, cut away the fabric behind the motif, leaving a margin of ⅛ in (3mm) next to the stitching.

Ribbon roses and **ribbon bows** are usually made from polyester satin ribbon in a wide range of colors, though some roses are made in printed nylon organza. Ribbon roses range in size from tiny ones, less than ⅜ in (10mm) across with glossy ribbon leaves, to 2in (5cm) in diameter. Hand-sew the roses to soft furnishings with a few tiny stitches. Ribbon bows come in many different widths, sometimes decorated with pearls at the center, and are attached in the same way.

Rosettes come ready-made in net, lace, or organza ribbon. **Swirls** are delicate circles of pleated voile with a stitched, wired edge. They can be twisted into rosettes and secured to an item with a few hand stitches.

Studs come in gold, silver, and oxidized metal finishes. They are available in a variety of shapes, including stars, and hearts, square, or round, and may be used to decorate a wide variety of soft furnishings.

There are two types of studs: the simple clamp stud and the riveted stud. Clamp studs come in a wider range of designs. They are very effective and easy to use, but are not as strong and secure as riveted studs and machine washing is not recommended.

Press the clamps (the pointed prongs) firmly through the fabric to the wrong side, then pull them toward the center of the stud to form claws, using fine pliers or tweezers. If your fabric is loosely woven, place a piece of tape at the back before inserting the stud. Riveted studs are generally small, round, and domed. They come in kits complete with a tool and clear instructions for easy application. They are usually machine washable and will withstand a great deal of wear and tear.

Tassels are available in all kinds of yarns, colors, shapes, and sizes. They are made and used as fashion trims and as home furnishing decorations. A vast array of single tassels is available, both in soft furnishing trimming departments and as fashion accessories: intricate key tassels, chunky tieback-size tassels, rough natural jute tassels, and silky dressing-gown style tassels in dazzling colors. Most come with a loop at the top for easy attaching, but some hang from the center of a cord rosette, which should be hand-sewn in place around the edge. Other novelties available are thread-covered balls on a loop.

feather

small ribbon roses

studs

studs

DISPLAYING PICTURES

Whether you have one, two, or several pictures to hang, it's worth planning the arrangement carefully so that you can view them with pleasure. Here are some guidelines to help you.

Large, bare walls. These look good with one very large or several quite large pictures; a couple of tiny pictures on a large wall can look lost. If you've got several small pictures, arrange them in a group for greater impact.

Plain, light walls. These are the easiest background to work with. They show off delicately toned pictures such as watercolors and pastels to advantage. Choose medium- or light-colored frames and mounts to match or contrast with the wall.

Plain, dark walls. These make a really dramatic backdrop for strong pictures and are ideal for very bold prints and richly colored oil paintings. Choose plain or ornate gilt or dark-colored frames and mounts in strong, complementary colors.

Walls covered with patterned wallpaper. These need careful thought, especially if the patterns are bold. Try a plain frame in one of the colors from the pattern, with a wide mount in the background color. This frame-and-mount combination helps the picture stand out from the wallpaper.

GROUPING PICTURES

Lay out your pictures on the floor beneath the wall you are hanging them on, and move them around until you find an arrangement you like. For a neat look, spaces between the pictures should be equal. See how the pictures are grouped on this page for ideas.

As a general guide, the center of the main picture should be just above eye level, with others grouped around it.

Coordinating pictures. When you are grouping pictures together, it helps to have a connecting theme, such as subject or color. Popular themes include seascapes, animals, portraits, and family snapshots. Use color to help coordinate a mixed collection of pictures. If the pictures themselves don't have similar colors, use matching frames and mounts.

Framing a collection. To add emphasis to a group of small pictures, you could set them inside a faux "frame" on the wall. This could be made from braid or a wallpaper border. Or you could paint or stencil designs linking them: try a ribbon or rope design, painted flowers, or ivy.

Pictures in a line. A group of pictures in different-sized frames often looks good hung with the top or bottom edges in a straight line. You can also position them with the centers on a straight line (as in the bottom row).

Pictures the same size. Arrange these in a square or rectangular group. Line up the pictures accurately and keep the vertical spaces equal.

Rectangular or square pictures. You can group these in two rows. The top row hangs from one horizontal line, while the bottom row stands on another. The sides of the outer pictures should also be aligned.

Working within a framework. Fill the corners of a stenciled or paneled frame with the largest pictures. Place smaller pictures at the outer edges, then fill in any gaps.

One large and six small pictures. You can arrange these symmetrically. Center a small picture on each side of the large one, and the others, equally spaced, above and below.

Set in a cross. Group pictures around an imaginary cross. Place the largest ones below the horizontal line, balanced by smaller ones above.

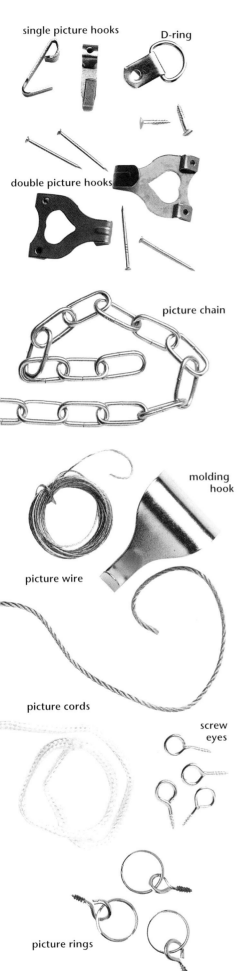

single picture hooks

D-ring

double picture hooks

picture chain

molding hook

picture wire

picture cords

screw eyes

picture rings

Hanging pictures

Here is a guide to the different fittings available for hanging pictures and how to use them.

D-rings. Rings in the shape of a D attached to a small metal plate. The plate is screwed into the back of the frame, about one-third of the way down from the top on each side of the picture. The picture cord or wire is threaded through the D-rings.

Ferrules. Metal tubes used to secure picture wire after threading it through a D-ring or screw eye.

Molding hooks. Specially shaped hooks designed for use with a picture rail. The hook fits onto the rail, and the picture is suspended from the hook without damaging the wall. Pictures hung using this method can be easily repositioned. You can hang them at different heights, simply by using shorter or longer pieces of picture wire.

Nails and screws. Very economical fixings for lightweight pictures only. You can simply fix a nail or screw into the wall and hang the picture from this. If you are using a screw, insert a plastic wall plug first.

Picture chain. Used to hang very heavy pictures and mirrors. It is sold by the yard (meter) by hardware stores and some picture framers. It's attached to the D-rings on the back of the picture with S-hooks.

Picture cord. Knotted to screw eyes at the back of the frame and hung on the picture hook. It is suitable for lightweight pictures.

Picture hooks. Shaped brass hooks that you fix to the wall with hardened steel pins. The holes in the hooks are aligned so that the pins enter the wall at an angle. This makes the fitting stronger and causes minimum damage to the wall.

Use a *single hook* for a very small picture and a *double hook* for a larger picture. Use two double hooks for a very heavy picture, to help equalize the load.

Picture wire. Used to hang medium-weight pictures. Unlike cord, it won't stretch or snap.

Screw eyes. An alternative to D-rings. They are screws that have a loop at the top to hold the cord or wire. They should be about two-thirds of the thickness of the frame.

S-hooks. Rings in the shape of a letter S used to attach picture chain to D-rings on the back of the picture. Never open a link of the chain instead.

USING CORD AND WIRE

FASTENING CORD

Measure the distance between the D-rings or screw eyes on the back of the frame and cut a piece of cord about 9in (23cm) longer than this. Knot one end of the cord to one D-ring or screw eye, then thread the other end through the other fixing. Pull the cord taut and knot it securely.

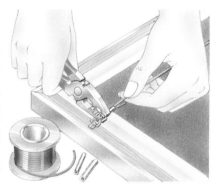

FASTENING PICTURE WIRE

Measure and cut the wire as in FASTENING CORD. Picture wire can't be knotted, so either thread it through the D-rings or screw eyes and twist each end of the wire back upon itself, or use ferrules as follows: thread one end of the wire through a ferrule, then through the D-ring or screw eye, and back through the ferrule. Use pliers to crimp the ferrule shut. Repeat to attach the other end of the wire to the frame, pulling it taut.

HANGING A PICTURE

1 MARKING THE POSITION
Hold the picture in position against the wall, and use a pencil to mark the position of the top corners. Remove the picture, then make a mark halfway between the two corner marks.

2 MEASURING THE DROP
Hold the picture by the center of the cord or wire so that the cord or wire is stretched taut. Measure the distance from the top of the taut wire to the top of the frame.

3 POSITIONING THE HOOK
Mark the wall this distance *below* the center mark. Fix the hook on the wall, so that the bottom of the hook rests on this mark. If you are hanging several pictures in a line, use a carpenter's level to check that all the hooks are level.

INDEX

Page numbers in *italics* refer to captions and illustrations

ACKNOWLEDGMENTS

Photographs:
Pages 1 Worldwide Syndication, 4 Elizabeth Whiting and Associates/Di Lewis, 5 Elrose Products, 45 Harlequin Fabrics, 81 Robert Harding Syndication/IPC Magazines/Homes & Gardens, 111 Elizabeth Whiting and Associates/Andreas von Einsiedel, 137 Crown Paints

7,8(t) Elrose Products, 8(b) Elizabeth Whiting and Associates/Di Lewis, 9(t) Elizabeth Whiting and Associates/David Cripps, (b) Elrose Products, 10(t) Elrose Products, (bl) Ariadne, Holland, 11 Robert Harding Syndication/Homes & Gardens/Jan Baldwin, 12(t) Robert Harding Syndication/Homes & Gardens/Graham Seazer, (b) Boys Syndication, 13(t) Houses and Interiors, (b) Elizabeth Whiting and Associates/June Buck, 14(t) Elizabeth Whiting and Associates/Rodney Hyett, (b) Worldwide Syndication, 15 Jon Bouchier, 16(t) Cristal Tiles, (bl) Cent Idées/Duffas/Schoumacher, (br) Robert Harding Syndication/IPC Magazines, 17 Jane Churchill, 18(t) Robert Harding Picture Library, (bl) Robert Harding Syndication/IPC Magazines/Homes & Gardens, (br) Elizabeth Whiting and Associates/Gary Chowanetz, 19 Robert Harding Syndication/Homes & Gardens/Michael Dunne, 20(tl) Marie Claire Idées/Schwartz/Chastres/Lancrenon, (tr) Robert Harding Syndication/Country Homes and Interiors/Tim Imrie, (b) Elizabeth Whiting and Associates/Spike Powell, 21 Forbo-Kingfisher, 22(t) Today Interiors, (b) Tabby Cat Designs, 23(tl,br) Eaglemoss Publications /Shona Wood, (tr) Elizabeth Whiting and Associates/Neil Lorimer, (bl) Arcaid/Lucinda Lambton, 24(t) Arthur Sanderson and Sons, (bl) Forbo-Kingfisher, (br)Eaglemoss Publications/Shona Wood, 25 Marie Claire Maison/Hussenot/Chastres/Comte/Roy, 26(t) Marie Claire Maison/Hussenot/Chastres/Comte/Roy, (b) Marie Claire Idées/Hussenot/Chastres, 27(t) The Garden Picture Library/Linda Burgess, (b) Eaglemoss Publications/Adrian Taylor, 28(t) Robert Harding Syndication/IPC Magazines/Ideal Home, (br) Marie Claire Maison/Hussenot/Chastres/Roy, (bl) Robert Harding Syndication/IPC Magazines/Country Homes & Interiors, 29 Elizabeth Whiting and Associates/Andreas von Einsiedel, 30(t) Worldwide Syndication, (b) Elizabeth Whiting and Associates/Victor Watts, 31(t) Elizabeth Whiting and Associates/Brian Harrison, (b) Elizabeth Whiting and Associates/Graham Henderson, 32(tl) Elizabeth Whiting and Associates/Michael Crockett, (tr) PWA International, (b) Crown Paints, 33 Ideal Standard, 34(t) Neil Holmes, (b) Cristal Tiles by H&R Johnson, 35(t) Boys Syndication, (b) Elizabeth Whiting and Associates/Brian Harrison, 36(t) Stovax Classic Fireplaces, (bl) Elizabeth Whiting and Associates/Tim Beddow, (br) Boys Syndication, 37 Ametex UK, 38(t) Dulux, (c) Modes et Travaux, (b) Robert Harding Syndication/IPC Magazines/Homes & Gardens, 39(t) Copley Decor Mouldings, (b) Robert Harding Syndication/IPC Magazines, 40(t) Richard Burbidge, (b) Robert Harding Syndication/IPC Magazines, 41 Elizabeth Whiting and Associates/Spike Powell, 42 Jon Bouchier, 43(t) Robert Harding Syndication/IPC Magazines/Homes & Gardens, (b) Elizabeth Whiting and Associates/Spike Powell, 44(tl) Elizabeth Whiting and Associates/Tom Leighton, (tr) Elizabeth Whiting and Associates/Di Lewis, (b) Robert Harding Syndication/IPC Magazines/Homes & Gardens, 47 Ariadne, Holland, 48(t) Robert Harding Syndication/IPC Magazines/Homes & Gardens, (bl) Marie Claire Idées/Vouvrais/Marsiglia, (br) Marks and Spencer, 49(t) Woodstock, (b) Elizabeth Whiting and Associates/Brian Harrison, 50(tl) Fired Earth, (tr) Elizabeth Whiting and Associates/Rodney Hyett, (b) Elizabeth Whiting and Associates/Di Lewis, 51 Christian Fischbacher/Charles Hammond, 52(t) Elizabeth Whiting and Associates/Spike Powell, (b) Elizabeth Whiting and Associates/Di Lewis, 53(t,br) Robert Harding Syndication/IPC Magazines, (bl) Elizabeth Whiting and Associates/Di Lewis, 54(tl) Laura Ashley, (tr) Marie Claire Idées/Fleurent/Lancrenon, (b) Elizabeth Whiting and Associates/Di Lewis, 55 Marie Claire Idées/Boucquet/Lancrenon, 56(c) Theo Woodham-Smith/Thomas Dare, (bl) Eaglemoss Publications/Adrian Taylor, (br) Modes et Travaux, (bc) Eaglemoss Publications/Adrian Taylor, 57(tl) Worldwide Syndication, (tr) Cope & Timmins Ltd, (bl) Robert Harding Syndication/IPC Magazines/Homes & Gardens, (br) Eaglemoss Publications/Adrian Taylor, 58(tl) Eaglemoss Publications/Adrian Taylor, (tr) Elizabeth Whiting and Associates/Michael Dunne, (b) The Design Archives, 59 Jahres Zeiten Verlag/Olaf Gollnek, 60(tl) Jahres Zeiten Verlag/Peter Adams, (tr) Robert Harding Syndication/Country Homes and Interiors/Chris Drake, (bl) Robert Harding Syndication/Ideal Home/Graham Rae, (br) Eaglemoss Publications/SteveTanner, 61 Robert Harding Picture Library, 62(t) Elizabeth Whiting and Associates/Andreas von Einsiedel, (b) Robert Harding Picture Library, 63(t) Elizabeth Whiting and Associates/Michael Dunne, (cl) Ariadne, Holland, (b) Eaglemoss Publications/Graham Rae, 64(tl) Eaglemoss Publications/Martin Chaffer, (tr) Robert Harding Picture Library, (b) Jane Churchill, 65 Robert Harding Syndication/IPC Magazines/Ideal Home, 66(t) Robert Harding Syndication/IPC Magazines/Country Homes & Interiors, (bl) Robert Harding Syndication/IPC Magazines/Ideal Home, (br) PWA International, 67 Robert Harding Syndication/IPC Magazines/Homes & Gardens, 68(t) Elizabeth Whiting and Associates/Rodney Hyett, (c) Robert Harding Syndication/IPC Magazines/Woman's Journal, (br) Boys Syndication, 69(t) Robert Harding Syndication/IPC Magazines/Homes & Gardens, (b) Marie Claire Idées/Giaume/Lancrenon, 70(t) Robert Harding Syndication/IPC Magazines/Homes & Gardens, (bl) Marie Claire Idées/Giaume/Digache, (br) Boys Syndication, 71 Robert Harding Syndication/Homes & Gardens/James Merrell, 72(tr) Marie Claire Idées/Hussenot/Chastres/Lancrenon, (cl) Ariadne, Holland, (br) Modes et Travaux, 73 Robert Harding Syndication/IPC Magazines/Homes & Gardens, 74(tl) Cliffhanger Glass Shelves, (tr) Robert Harding Syndication/IPC Magazines/Homes & Gardens, (b) Marie Claire Idées/Schwartz/Lancrenon, 75(t) Robert Harding Syndication/IPC Magazines/Country Homes & Interiors, (r) Marie Claire Idées/Chabaneix, 76(t) Worldwide Syndication, (b) Robert Harding Syndication/IPC Magazines/Country Homes and Interiors, 77 Cent Idées/Doucet, 78(t) Sue Atkinson, (b) Cent Idées/Boys, 79(t) Cent Idées, (b) Eaglemoss Publications/John Suett, 80(tl) Elizabeth Whiting and Associates/Di Lewis, (tr) Rubena Grigg, (b) Cent Idées/Mae/Mehé, 83(t) Elizabeth Whiting and Associates/Jon Bouchier, (b) Elizabeth Whiting and Associates/Michael Nicholson, 84(t) Arcaid/Richard Bryant, (b) John Hollingshead, 85(t) Elizabeth Whiting and Associates/Jerry Tubby, (c) Elizabeth Whiting and Associates/Tom Leighton, (b) Arcaid/Annet Held, 86(t) Robert Harding Syndication/IPC Magazines (bl) Houses and Interiors, (br) Elizabeth Whiting and Associates/Neil Lorimer, 87(t) Elizabeth Whiting and Associates/Victor Watts, (br) Eaglemoss Publications/Steve Tanner, 88(t) Elizabeth Whiting and Associates/Andreas von Einsiedel, (b) Elizabeth Whiting and Associates/Dennis Stone, 89(t) Laura Ashley, (tr) Elizabeth Whiting and Associates/Michael Dunne, (bl) Robert Harding Syndication/IPC Magazines, 90(t,br) Robert Harding Syndication/IPC Magazines, (bl) Laura Ashley, 91 Robert Harding Syndication/IPC Magazines/Homes & Gardens, 92(cl) Elizabeth Whiting and Associates/Andreas von Einsiedel, (bl) The Garden Picture Library/Ann Kelley, (br) Ikea, 93(t) Elizabeth Whiting and Associates/Di Lewis, (b) Elizabeth Whiting and Associates/Tom Leighton, 94(tl) Friars Goose Ltd, (tr) Jane Churchill, (b) Arthur Sanderson and Sons, 95 Worldwide Syndication, 96(t) Habitat, (b) Ikea, 97(t) Robert Harding Syndication/IPC Magazines/Ideal Home, (bl) Eaglemoss Publications/Simon Page-Ritchie, (br) Robert Harding Syndication/IPC Magazines/Homes & Gardens, 98(tl) Robert Harding Syndication/IPC Magazines/Homes & Gardens, (tr) Ingrid Mason Picture Library/Marie-Louise Avery, (b) Robert Harding Syndication/IPC Magazines/Country Homes & Interiors, 99 Romo Fabrics, 100(t) Robert Harding Syndication/IPC Magazines/Homes & Gardens, (b) Crown Paints, 101(t) Robert Harding Syndication/IPC Magazines/Ideal Home, (b) Robert Harding Syndication/IPC Magazines/Homes & Gardens, 102(t) Robert Harding Syndication/IPC Magazines/Homes & Gardens, (b) Robert Harding Syndication/IPC Magazines/Ideal Home, 103 Today Interiors, 104(c) Eaglemoss Publications/Graham Rae, (b) Robert Harding Syndication/IPC Magazines/Country Homes & Interiors, 104-105 Ariadne, Holland, 105(bl) The Merchant Tiler, (br) Robert Harding Syndication/IPC Magazines, 106(t) Dorma, (bl) Cristal Tiles, (br) Robert Harding Syndication/IPC Magazines/Country Homes & Interiors, 107 Elizabeth Whiting and Associates/Tim Beddow, 108 Robert Harding Syndication/IPC Magazines/Homes & Gardens, 109(t) Robert Harding Syndication/IPC Magazines/Homes & Gardens, (b) Elizabeth Whiting and Associates/Victor Watts, 110(t) PWA International, (bl) Robert Harding Syndication/IPC Magazines/Ideal Home, (br) Robert Harding Syndication/IPC Magazines/Homes & Gardens, 113 Arthur Sanderson and Sons, 114(t) Eaglemoss Publications/SteveTanner, (b) Laura Ashley, 115(t) Elizabeth Whiting and Associates/Clive Helm, (bl) Elizabeth Whiting and Associates/Tim Beddow, (br) Elizabeth Whiting and Associates/Andreas von Einsiedel, 116(t) Robert Harding Syndication/IPC Magazines/Country Homes & Interiors, (bl) Warner Fabrics, (br) Eaglemoss Publications/SteveTanner, 117 Designers Guild, 118(tr) Laura Ashley, (bl) Eaglemoss Publications/Adrian Taylor, 119(t) Biggie Best, (bl) Jane Churchill, (br) Worldwide Syndication, 120(tl) Eric Crichton, (tr) Elizabeth Whiting and Associates/Enzo Minnino, (bl) Tabby Cat Designs, (br) Eaglemoss Publications/Adrian Taylor, 121 Robert Harding Syndication/IPC Magazines/Homes & Gardens, 122(t) Robert Harding Syndication/IPC Magazines/Country Homes & Interiors, (b) Kirsch, 123(t) David Parmiter, (b) Marie Claire Idées/Chabaneix, 124(t) Habitat, (bl) Ariadne, Holland, (br) Robert Harding Syndication/IPC Magazines/Homes & Gardens, 125 Robert Harding Syndication/IPC Magazines/Homes & Gardens, 126(t) Woolpit Interiors, (b) Robert Harding Syndication/IPC Magazines/Homes & Gardens, 127(t) Elizabeth Whiting and Associates/Andreas von Einsiedel, (b) Insight, London/Michelle Garrett, 128 Robert Harding Syndication/IPC Magazines/Homes & Gardens, 129 Robert Harding Syndication/Homes & Gardens/Trevor Richards, 130(t) Robert Harding Syndication/Ideal Home/Steve Haskins, (b) Robert Harding Syndication/Homes & Gardens/Chris Drake, 131(t) Robert Harding Syndication/Country Homes and Interiors/Nadia McKenzie, (b) Robert Harding Syndication/Homes & Gardens/Arthur Hunt, 132(t) Marie Claire Idées/Fleurent/Chastres, (bl) Genevieve Lethu, (br) Ametex, 133 Romo Fabrics, 134(t) Robert Harding Syndication/IPC Magazines/Homes & Gardens, (b) Marks and Spencer, 135(t) Jane Churchill, (b) PWA International, 136(tl,b) Ariadne, Holland, (tr) Eaglemoss Publications/John Suett, 140, 142 Eaglemoss Publications/Adrian Taylor, 144 Eaglemoss Publications/SteveTanner, 145,148 Eaglemoss Publications/Adrian Taylor, 153(l) Eaglemoss Publications/John Suett, (r) Eaglemoss Publications/Adrian Taylor, 154 Eaglemoss Publications/John Suett, 155 Eaglemoss Publications/Simon Page-Ritchie, 156-7 Eaglemoss Publications/Adrian Taylor, 158 Eaglemoss Publications/Simon Page-Ritchie, 159 Dulux, 160 Eaglemoss Publications/Adrian Taylor, 161 Eaglemoss Publications/artin Norris, 162 Eaglemoss Publications/John Suett, 164 Eaglemoss Publications, 165 Acorn Adaptable Pasting Table, 170 Today Interiors, 174 Eaglemoss Publications/Adrian Taylor, 175 Crown Paints, 183 Eaglemoss Publications/Adrian Taylor, 184 (tl,bl,r) Eaglemoss Publications/SteveTanner, (cl) Eaglemoss Publications/Simon Page-Ritchie, 185 Eaglemoss Publications/Steve Tanner, 187 Eaglemoss Publications/Adrian Taylor.

Illustrations:
111, 138-145 Kuo Kang Chen, 149 Aziz Khan, 150-1 Kuo Kang Chen, 152 Eaglemoss Publications, 153(t) Sally Holmes, (b) Eaglemoss Publications, 154-169 Kuo Kang Chen, 170-1 Eugene Fleury, 172-177 Kuo Kang Chen, 178-180 Eugene Fleury, 182-3 Kuo Kang Chen, 184-5 Sally Holmes, 186 Kuo Kang Chen.